The Betrayal of Richard III

The Betrayal of Richard III

V.B. LAMB

with an Introduction and Notes by
P.W. HAMMOND

ALAN SUTTON PUBLISHING LIMITED

First published in 1959

This revised edition first published in the United Kingdom in 1990 by
Alan Sutton Publishing Ltd · Phoenix Mill · Far Thrupp · Stroud · Gloucestershire

Reprinted 1996

British Library Cataloguing in Publication Data

Lamb, V.B.
    The betrayal of Richard III.
    1. England. Richard III, King of England
    I. Title
    942.046092

    ISBN 0-86299-778-X

Typeset in 10/12 Bembo.
Typesetting and origination by
Alan Sutton Publishing Limited.
Printed in Great Britain by
Guernsey Press Limited.

CONTENTS

LIST OF ILLUSTRATIONS

ACKNOWLEDGEMENTS

Acknowledgements and thanks for permission to reproduce photographs are due to the Ashmolean Museum (3), British Museum (6), Society of Antiquaries (10, 11), Victoria and Albert Museum (12). Plates 1, 2 and 5 are reproduced by gracious permission of Her Majesty the Queen.

Thanks are also due to Dr Pamela Tudor-Craig for help over the 'Broken Sword' portrait, to David Scuffam for his excellent drawings used as chapter endings, and to Julian Rowe for the (equally excellent) last drawing and for the magnificent reconstruction of Fotheringhay Castle.

THE HOUSES OF YORK AND LANCASTER

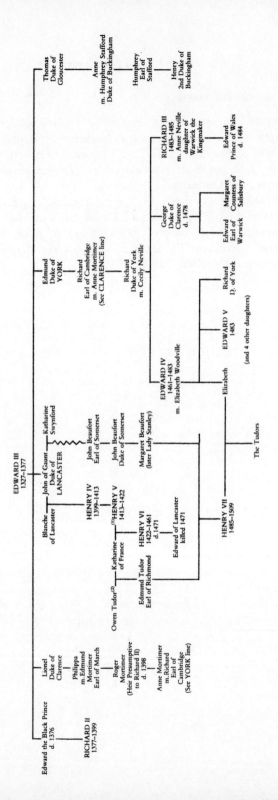

INTRODUCTION

T his book was written in 1959, over thirty years ago. It immediately took its place in a long line of books, briefly described by the author in chapter XI, which pointed out the defects in the traditional picture of the last Plantagenet king, Richard III. It is totally and unashamedly written from the 'reformist' point of view, which is no very bad thing, since there are many brief histories of this period which take the opposite view of Richard of Gloucester, and there is room for a book as well written as this one, which puts a case in favour of Richard – a book which is moreover a very clear description of a very complex subject.

When this book was written, few were apparently interested in the late Middle Ages. It is difficult now to think back to that time, when very little was being published on the period, and to compare it with the veritable explosion of books published in the last twenty-five years: in 1976 indeed, the late Middle Ages were described by Dr Wolffe as one of the 'great growth periods in English historical studies'.[1] When *The Betrayal of Richard III* was published the growth period was in fact about to begin, Mrs Lamb being one of the pioneers. The biography of Richard III by P.M. Kendall, which, while it may not have started the growth, certainly helped, was published in 1955, and his less successful *Warwick the Kingmaker* followed in 1957. Work was of course continuing in the universities in the 'quiet' years. K.B. MacFarlane at Oxford had been working on fifteenth century topics since 1925, and in fact wrote the chapter on the Lancastrian kings in the *Cambridge Medieval History*, Volume 8, in 1936. Professor Charles Ross, one of his pupils, quotes a statement that MacFarlane inspired 'the only school that fifteenth century historiography has had'.[2] It was indeed to a real extent his pupils who carried out, or in their turn inspired, much of the subsequent work. There have been general works on the political life of the late fifteenth century (for example *The Wars of the Roses* by Charles Ross), there have been biographies of the main protagonists (Henry VI, Edward IV, Richard III and Henry VII), and many volumes of the proceedings of numerous conferences, as well as innumerable articles in historical journals. There have also been new editions of some of the source materials, for example the *Paston Letters*, the *Crowland Chronicle* and Dominic Mancini's report. The published editions include the first ever complete edition of British Library Harleian Manuscript 433. This was based on a complete transcription of the English portions made by Mrs Lamb over four arduous years. She also made name and place indexes to these portions.[3]

This explosion of knowledge has in some ways changed perceptions of Richard III. Most historians would now accept Mrs Lamb's common-sense view of Richard as a man, of his guiltlessness at least of the crimes he has been accused of committing before he became king, and of his desire for justice. Interestingly her claim (p. xi) that a modern jury would consider that there was no case for Richard III to answer has been borne out in a televised staging of his trial on a charge of murdering his nephews.[4] However, the increase in knowledge has also meant that some of her statements need to be qualified in the light of recent research. The notes in this new edition are intended to update it without altering the form of Mrs Lamb's references or detracting from her own trenchant and uncompromising prose, and to give it the new lease of life which it deserves.

P.W.H.
April 1990

REFERENCES

1. In a review of Charles Ross, *Edward IV*, in *English Historical Review*, vol. 91, p. 374.
2. Introduction to *Patronage, Pedigree and Power in Later Medieval England*, edited by Charles Ross, 1979, p. 8, quoting Dr Delloyd Guth.
3. For the books mentioned above see Part Two of the Bibliography.
4. Richard Drewett and Mark Redhead, *The Trial of Richard III*, Gloucester, 1984.

FOREWORD

*T*he purpose of this book is to examine very briefly the foundations on which one of the most famous legends in English history has been built.

I do not claim to throw any fresh light on the mystery which surrounds Richard III, neither do I propose to make an exhaustive survey of his life and times. Rather do I wish to trace the growth of the traditional legend from its conception through the main accepted sources, and to emphasize the doubtful nature of the basis upon which this elaborate and apparently circumstantial story was built – a story which has been widely accepted as incontrovertible over a period of nearly five hundred years.

In fact, the evidence for the traditional picture of Richard is of such a flimsy and suspect nature that a modern jury would, I think, rightly consider that on it there is no case to answer.

V.B. LAMB
1959

PRELUDE
TO DISASTER

I

EDWARD, BY THE GRACE OF GOD

*W*hen Edward IV died at Westminster on April 9th, 1483 he had been King of England for twenty one years and nine months with a short intermission in 1470–71. He inherited his claim to the throne from his father, Richard Duke of York, killed at the battle of Wakefield on December 30th, 1460, and there is no doubt that this claim was valid in law. The House of York was descended through the female line from Lionel of Clarence, third surviving (effectually the second) son of Edward III, whereas the House of Lancaster which it superseded derived its descent from John of Gaunt, the fourth son of the same King, and owed its possession of the throne to the usurpation of Henry of Bolingbroke, who had deposed his cousin Richard II, whom he imprisoned in Pontefract Castle where the unfortunate King met a diversely reported but undoubtedly unpleasant end, while Henry had himself crowned as Henry IV.

In 1460 the throne was nominally occupied by Henry's grandson, Henry VI, who had succeeded as an infant of nine months, and after a long and disturbed minority had grown into a saintly but feeble-witted man, quite unfitted to govern a turbulent realm. As a result the government of the country was in the hands of his wife, Margaret of Anjou, and her successive favourites, the Dukes of Suffolk and Somerset, whose relations with the Queen gave rise to considerable scandal. It was generally thought that her only son, Edward of Lancaster, was in fact the son of Somerset, a rumour which received considerable impetus when King Henry, on being informed of the birth of an heir, remarked that it must have been through the agency of the Holy Ghost.[1] However pleasing such divine intervention might be to the saintly King, it was hardly calculated to inspire confidence in his subjects, a large proportion of whom were bitterly discontented with the oppressive rule of the foreign woman and her lovers. During the 1450s the country seethed with discontent and sporadic outbreaks of civil strife, and an increasingly large number of the people began to look to the Duke of York as the rightful King of England and their only hope of stable government. These hopes were dashed when the Duke was killed in a fight with Queen Margaret's army at Wakefield, to be swiftly revived in the person of his son, Edward.

Edward was the eldest of the sons of Richard of York who survived to reach manhood, the other two being George, afterwards Duke of Clarence, and Richard, afterwards Duke of Gloucester. Their mother was Cecily Neville, daughter of Ralph Earl of Westmorland and aunt of Richard Earl of Warwick later to be known to history as the Kingmaker. Edward was liberally endowed to be a leader of men and a lover of women. Six feet four inches tall, with the frame of a giant, he was dazzlingly fair and famous for his good looks throughout Europe. He was also, when he chose to exert himself, a brilliant commander and a shrewd man of business.

At the time of his father's death, when it seemed that the White Rose of York had withered past revival, he was not quite nineteen and was engaged in raising an army in Wales to go to the Duke of York's assistance. Within six weeks of receiving the news of the disaster at Wakefield he had won the battle of Mortimer's Cross and received a delirious welcome to London, where he was formally offered the Crown in the great hall of his mother's house, Baynard's Castle. Before another two months had passed he had smashed the Lancastrian armies at Towton, and on June 29th he was solemnly crowned King of England. Margaret of Anjou with her precious son took refuge in France, where she received a restrained welcome from Louis XI, who showed no enthusiasm for the cause of a penniless and dethroned relative.

Edward was firmly seated on the throne to which he had every right, and for three years the sun of York blazed in an almost cloudless sky. The Lancastrian nobility was scattered, either dead or in exile with the luckless Margaret. Edward had the powerful support of his cousin the Earl of Warwick to whom, after his own genius for command, he to a large extent owed his throne. If he felt any resentment at the obligation no rift was apparent between them, and when the important question of a suitable wife for the King of

England arose it was to Warwick that the negotiations were entrusted.

Edward's marriage was a matter of the utmost importance. On it, in the eyes of Europe, depended the stability of his newly-won throne and the dynastic future of his house. He could, and did, take his extra-marital relaxations where he chose, but his marriage was something which could not be trifled with. Several royal alliances were under consideration, among them being Isabella of Spain and the Princess Bona of Savoy, sister-in-law of Louis of France, the latter being favoured by Warwick. Unfortunately for the peace of England and the future of the House of York the most important factor to be reckoned with was Edward's own temperament. Not only was he immensely attractive to women and accustomed to getting his own way with them; he was also extremely susceptible, and where a woman was concerned his natural shrewdness seems to have been lacking. Also he was very young and very successful. At twenty he was the victor in two pitched battles against superior odds, he was a king, and the idol of his people. It would hardly be surprising if in his own mind he was a law unto himself with the conviction that the King could do no wrong.

Whatever the reasons it was at this critical moment, when the question of his marriage was being gravely discussed by his Council, that he committed an act of supreme folly which was destined to destroy the House of York. On a hunting trip to Grafton, the home of Richard Woodville, Baron Rivers, he met the eldest daughter of his host, the widow of Sir John Grey, who had lost his life at the battle of St Albans fighting for the Lancastrians. Elizabeth Woodville, Lady Grey, was an amazingly beautiful woman some six years older than the King; the moment Edward set eyes on her he fell desperately in love and determined to have her no matter what the cost. This proved to be very much higher than that which he was accustomed to pay on these occasions. The lady, probably with a shrewd sense of her own value, firmly refused to become his mistress. It was marriage or nothing. Edward, frantic at this unusual check to his desires, threw overboard the foreign marriage, his Council, and the Earl of Warwick, and on May 1st, 1464, very secretly at Grafton, he married the beautiful Elizabeth, and by that rather furtive little May Day ceremony he doomed his dynasty and his whole family to extinction.

Five months elapsed before Edward plucked up courage to tell his

Council what he had done, during which time Warwick continued his negotiations for a foreign bride for his King and cousin. When at last it was no longer possible to conceal the disastrous marriage the reaction was immediate. Warwick was furious at having been made to look a fool before the courts of Europe, and never forgave his cousin. Edward's other supporters deeply resented this marriage with the daughter of one Lancastrian and the widow of another, both of obscure origin, for Lord Rivers was of very new creation and his chief claim to importance had so far lain in his marriage, as her second husband, to Jacqueline of Luxembourg, sister of the Count of St Pol and the widow of Henry V's brother the Duke of Bedford, a lady of doubtful reputation which included a suspicion of dabbling in sorcery and the black arts. A Queen with such antecedents could never be acceptable to the proud Yorkist nobility, but added to these disadvantages Elizabeth Woodville was one of a numerous family of brothers and sisters, all ambitious and all of them determined to make the most of the amazing piece of good fortune which had raised their sister to the throne. There were also her two sons by her first marriage, who in due course became candidates for honours which should more properly have gone to others.

In a very short time Edward had given all his Queen's male relations huge estates and positions which made them the equals of the highest in the land. Her father was made Earl Rivers while her sisters were married to leading members of the old aristocracy who had to submit, but who regarded this influx of Lancastrian upstarts with bitter hatred which time did nothing to assuage. The arrogance of the new family still further exacerbated the outraged feelings of the old nobility, while their rapacity made them universally hated by the commons. The wound was never healed, and never again was Edward to enjoy the unanimous support of his followers. Intrigue and jealousies grew and flourished, and as Habington wrote in his *Life of Edward IV*: '. . . the outward face of the court was full of the beauty of delight and majesty while the inward was all rotten with discord and envy'.

The unfortunate marriage had cast a shadow over the bright future of York which was never to lift, and as time went by grew ever deeper and more threatening until it swallowed up the glory on an August day on Bosworth field twenty-one years later.

In 1470 Edward's own particular chickens came home to roost

with the rebellion of his cousin and former friend the Earl of Warwick, supported by George of Clarence who had married, against Edward's wishes, Isobel, the elder of Warwick's two daughters, and who found the pretensions of the Woodville clan as intolerable as did his father-in-law. Warwick and Clarence fled to France where they joined forces with Margaret of Anjou and entered into a pact by which they agreed to help her to regain the English throne for her husband and son, cementing the alliance by the betrothal of Warwick's younger daughter Anne Neville to Edward of Lancaster.

With ships and men provided by King Louis, Warwick and Clarence invaded England, forcing Edward to flee the country with his youngest brother Richard of Gloucester and a handful of friends, in such haste that they arrived in Flanders, where their sister Margaret was married to Duke Charles the Bold of Burgundy, in a state of penury. In England Warwick dragged the imbecile Henry from his devotions in the Tower, where he had led a congenial life since his capture after the battle of Towton, suitably attended by a retinue of priests and servants, decked him in the royal robes, paraded him about London and declared him King. Edward and Richard were attainted, while Elizabeth Woodville, who had taken sanctuary at Westminster, there gave birth to the long hoped for son whose inheritance at that moment seemed to be more than doubtful.

Adversity however had a good effect on Edward. He threw off the sloth of the past years which had enabled his enemies to drive him into exile, raised a small force with the help of his sister and her husband, and accompanied by the faithful Richard of Gloucester he set sail for England in March 1471, landing in Yorkshire. From thence he executed a lightning march southwards and in a matter of six weeks had recaptured London, defeated and killed Warwick at the battle of Barnet, and three weeks later finally annihilated the main Lancastrian army at Tewkesbury where Edward of Lancaster was, according to the contemporary *Fleetwood Chronicle* and the *Paston Letters*, slain in the battle. The *Paston Letters* contain a list headed 'Ded in the Feld'. The first name is that of Edward of Lancaster.[2]

Most of the leading Lancastrians either died at Tewkesbury or were executed immediately afterwards, but among the few who escaped were the Earl of Pembroke and his nephew the young Earl of Richmond, aged fifteen, who was later to become Henry VII. On his father's side Henry was the grandson of Owen Tudor, who had secretly married the widow of Henry V, and his mother, Margaret Beaufort, was a descendant of John of Gaunt by his mistress, Katherine Swinford, who had married Edmund Tudor, Earl of Richmond. After the now childless Henry VI she and her son alone represented the Lancastrian strain of the blood of Edward III, albeit illegitimately.[3] Henry Tudor fled to Brittany where he led a precarious existence for the next fifteen years.

The victor of Tewkesbury returned in triumph to London and shortly afterwards Henry VI, who had been returned to his seclusion in the Tower, was found dead. The account given out by Edward said that he had died of grief at the news of Tewkesbury and the death of his son; this explanation may well be true, and his death was certainly very convenient, but it is equally likely that he was murdered as the result of a decision taken by Edward in Council to obviate any possibility of further disturbances on his behalf. This explanation is borne out by a cryptic reference to his death in the near-contemporary *Chronicle of Croyland*.

Edward was now firmly restored to his throne and reunited to his family. The birth of a son after a succession of four daughters had made the position of the Queen and her family stronger than ever, if not more popular. Clarence, who had become reconciled to his brother before the battle of Barnet was in no way deterred by his own record from voicing his dislike of the Woodvilles, and the upheavals of the past year had done nothing to reconcile the discordant elements which composed the Court. True, the Woodville family had lost two of its members during the recent disturbances; Earl Rivers and his son John Woodville had been captured by insurgents near Chepstow. Among the rebels' demands to the King was that the hated family should be removed from their positions of influence, but the capture of Rivers and his son gave them the opportunity for more direct action which they were not slow to seize, and the two Woodvilles were summarily executed. John Woodville was particularly hated for his marriage at the age of twenty to the enormously wealthy dowager Duchess of Norfolk who was in her eighties. It was known as the diabolical marriage, and had shocked the entire country.

There were, however, plenty of Woodvilles left. The new Earl Rivers was the only member of the family who seems to have achieved some degree of popularity. He was a man of culture, a patron of the arts, and was instrumental in establishing Caxton and his printing press at Westminster. Of the Queen's other surviving brothers one, Lionel, was Bishop of Salisbury while the other, Edward, and her younger son Richard had received military rank and generous grants of lands. Her elder son by her first marriage, Sir Thomas Grey, had been created Marquis of Dorset and was one of the King's favourite companions on his less reputable excursions, while five of her sisters had been married into the great houses of Buckingham, Essex, Kent, Arundel, and Huntingdon. The Woodville roots had spread far and wide.

In 1475 Edward embarked on a full-scale expedition against France. He had received a request for help from his brother-in-law, Charles the Bold of Burgundy, in the perpetual state of war which existed between Burgundy and France. Edward owed Charles a considerable debt for the help he had received in regaining his own kingdom and was not in a very strong position to refuse the Duke's appeal. Also a foreign diversion which would occupy his own nobles with matters other than their own squabbles had some appeal for the King. Finally a war with France was popular in the country and would serve to unite those of his subjects who might still hanker after the lost Lancastrian cause. The English had felt bitterly the loss of their French conquests and were very ready to follow their English hero in an attempt to regain the lost crown of France. This was very necessary, for large sums of money were needed to fit out the expedition which had to be raised by taxation.

In order to raise this money Edward used a device which was euphemistically called a 'benevolence'.[4] This form of taxation was supposed to be a free gift to the King from his loving subjects; in fact there was nothing free about it. It was a capital levy assessed on every man's ability to pay, the King having a very shrewd idea of what that ability was through an intricate network of spies who kept him informed of the financial status of his subjects. Edward was not above using his sex appeal to increase the contributions; one old lady gave him more than he asked for 'for the sake of his lovely face'. The gratified King thereupon kissed her and the contribution was promptly doubled!

One way and another, by kisses or curses, a large sum of money was raised, and in July 1475 the King crossed the Channel with his two brothers and the largest army that had ever left the shores of England, followed by the high hopes and patriotic fervour of the whole nation. Two months later it was back in England without having drawn a sword. Edward had found Charles the Bold an unreliable and irresponsible ally whose performance fell far short of his promises. The subtle Louis of France took advantage of the brothers-in-law's disagreements to suggest to Edward that hard cash was a better proposition than the conquest of a devastated country, which, even if won, would be a constant source of trouble and expense to hold. The two kings met at Picquigny where a treaty was signed whereby Louis betrothed his eldest son to the Princess Elizabeth of York and paid Edward the sum of seventy-five thousand gold crowns cash down, with the promise of a pension of fifty thousand crowns annually. Edward's nobles also received handsome presents and annuities, the largest sums going to William Lord Hastings, Edward's Chamberlain and closest friend. Edward called the annuity a tribute and the French called it a bribe, so that everyone was satisfied at the somewhat inglorious ending to the campaign except the Duke of Gloucester who expressed the deepest disgust at the whole transaction, and presumably the people of England who were the poorer by their benevolences and who had been cheated of their dreams of victory.[5]

After this not very impressive campaign the victor of Towton, Barnet and Tewkesbury sought no more military glory. For some time rich living and indulgence had dulled the once famous beauty of the Sun of York. Edward was putting on weight, and the life which he led with Dorset, Hastings, and his other cronies began to tell on his health. He was now the father of a second son by his Queen who seems to have condoned his infidelities if she did not actually connive at them. His mistresses were legion, the *maitresse en titre* being Jane Shore who appears to have been generally popular at Court and even a friend of the Queen.[6]

During these years the star of the Woodvilles burned ever more brightly. The young Prince of Wales was given his own establishment at Ludlow under the tutelage of Earl Rivers, his maternal uncle, and his half-brother, Richard Grey.[7] His household was composed of persons favouring the Woodville faction, so that he was entirely under the influence of his mother's family, an arrangement which must have caused considerable misgiving to his future subjects. But Edward was master in his own house and while he chose to favour his Queen's family there was nothing that the old nobility could do but swallow their resentment as best they might.

The exception was George of Clarence, who lost no opportunity in voicing his dislike of his sister-in-law's relations. Edward had shown great patience in his dealings with Clarence; he had forgiven him for his outrageous treachery at the time of Warwick's rebellion, and he had put up with his endless trouble-making about the Court and his overweening pride and conceit. In 1478, however, after a series of misdemeanours which included tampering with the King's justice, his own folly combined with the enmity of the Woodvilles brought about his downfall. He was tried and found guilty on a charge of high treason, which seems to have included some slanderous statements against the King or his family which have never been clearly defined. After the death sentence had been passed, Edward still hesitated to sign the warrant, and it was not till a month later, following a deputation from parliament asking that the sentence should be carried out, that Edward finally gave orders that his brother should be privately put to death in the Tower. There is no record of the manner of his death, but it is unlikely that he was really drowned in a butt of Malmsey. However he died he certainly deserved what he got, having worn out Edward's long patience.

The sands were running low for Edward himself. In 1480 the Scots repudiated their treaties with England and in 1481 an expedition under the Duke of Gloucester crossed the border, took the towns of Berwick and Edinburgh, and imposed terms on the King of Scotland.

A year later the King of France also broke his treaties, withdrew the 'tribute', and betrothed the Dauphin to the heiress of Burgundy. Edward was furious, and set about planning another expedition to France, but before his plans were far advanced he caught a chill which, in the impaired state of his health, proved fatal. On his deathbed he appointed his absent brother Richard of Gloucester sole protector of the realm and guardian of his children.[8] He made a pathetic attempt to heal the jealousies and animosities of years by an appeal to those nobles of the different factions who were standing round his bed to forget their differences and join in the support of his son. Then he died, just three weeks before his forty-first birthday.

THE KING'S BROTHER

*R*ichard Plantagenet was the youngest surviving child of Richard, Duke of York and Cecily Neville. In looks, as in character, he seems to have resembled his father, being something under middle height and darker than his two brothers, Edward and George, who both inherited the Neville fairness and length of limb. There was no suggestion made at any time during his lifetime that he was in any way deformed, though a reference to him in early childhood contained in a rhyming account of the Duke of York's family by an anonymous writer, tells the reader that he 'liveth yet', which seems to imply that there had been some doubt of his survival (*Annals, William of Worcester*).

However, survive he did, though little is known of his early childhood except that he was born at Fotheringhay on October 2nd, 1452, that at the age of seven he was captured at Ludlow by the Lancastrians together with his mother, his brother George and his sister Margaret, and that in the following autumn of 1460 all four were once more at liberty and awaiting the return of the Duke of York from Ireland in the London lodgings of John Paston, where their elder brother Edward visited them every day (*Paston Letters*).

By the end of the year the Yorkist cause was so much in the ascendant that the family was once more installed in its London home, Baynard's Castle, but it was there that news of the disaster at Wakefield reached the Duchess of York. Her two younger sons, George and Richard, were immediately put on board a Flemish ship which was about to sail from the Thames and sent out of danger into the custody of Philip the Good, Duke of Burgundy, whose son, Charles the Bold, was later to marry their elder sister, Margaret of York. Having lost his father, a brother (Edmund Earl of Rutland), and an uncle (the Earl of Salisbury), to say nothing of the bright future which so recently had seemed assured to his family, the months which the eight-year-old boy spent in exile in Burgundy must have rocked the foundations of his whole world, and though it was only five months before the news of his brother Edward's victory at Towton called him and his brother George home again, the time spent among strangers must have been one which left its mark on both children.

They returned to England to be welcomed by a triumphant elder brother, the hero of his followers and the idol of the people, who had already acclaimed him King. Good looks, brave deeds, fame and popularity – Edward had them all, and here indeed was a figure to dazzle the eyes and win the devotion of a small boy, too young to feel the jealousy which may well have lurked in the heart of his brother George, four years older, and of a very different temperament. Certainly Richard's devotion and loyalty to his brother throughout their joint lives was unquestioned in spite of severe trials, particularly in later years when the idol's feet of clay became distressingly apparent, and the golden young warrior had been lost in the debauched and prematurely aged man.

From the first, Edward showed marked affection for his youngest brother. Shortly after his coronation in the summer of 1461 he created him Duke of Gloucester, while at the same time George was made Duke of Clarence and both brothers Knights of the Garter.[9]

About this time Richard seems to have entered the household of his powerful cousin the Earl of Warwick, where, following the custom of the time, he was educated in the courtly graces and martial training considered essential to the son of a noble house. His companions were to become his lifelong friends, Francis Lovell, Richard Ratcliffe, and other scions of the great houses of the north at Warwick's castle of Middleham in Wensleydale. Here also he had the society of Warwick's two daughters, Isobel and Anne, and it seems at least probable that his love for the latter, whom he was later to marry, began in these early days of childhood.

At the age of fourteen Richard took his place at his brother's court, and although practically nothing is known of his attitude towards the already uneasy undercurrents which ebbed and flowed between the Queen's family and the old aristocracy, it is certain that Warwick failed to undermine his loyalty to Edward, successful though the earl was with his brother Clarence. Edward must have been aware of the reliance which he could place on the boy, for not a year passed but Richard received further marks of his brother's affection and trust in the shape of grants, lands, honours, and titles. At the age of sixteen, in addition to many lesser posts, he held those of Lord High Admiral and Chief Constable of England, as well as Chief Justice of the Marches of Wales. There is nothing during these years that tells us anything of Richard – nothing but the fact of his unshakeable loyalty to his brother and of Edward's evident affection for him.

In 1470 came Warwick's rebellion, and Richard followed his brother and King into exile, while Warwick and Clarence enjoyed their brief triumph. He returned to England with the little force which was all that Edward could muster for his desperate gamble to regain the lost crown. It was Richard who rode into Clarence's camp near Banbury and finally talked the already wavering George into making his peace with Edward, thereby earning himself for the second time the title of 'false fleeting perjured Clarence'.[10] It was Richard, not yet eighteen, who led the right wing of Edward's army at Barnet with brilliant success and a superb display of personal courage. It was Richard who surpassed his own performance at Tewkesbury, and who rode into London at his brother's right hand to receive a conqueror's ovation from the populace. The two brothers spent only one night – that of May 21st – in London before leaving next morning to quell a subsidiary rising in Kent. During this night Henry VI is said to have been killed in the Tower, though the date is by no means certain. John Warkworth chronicles the murder on that night, adding by the way that the Duke of Gloucester was, with others, in the Tower, an insinuation which means very little as the whole Court would have been there, the Duke of Gloucester fully occupied with preparations for the morrow's departure, and the hundred and one matters with which the commander of an army has to deal in the middle of a campaign. If Henry was indeed murdered, as the result of a decision taken for reasons of policy by Edward in Council, then Richard, as a member of the Council, must bear his share of the collective guilt, but there is no reason to suppose that he had a more personal connection with the crime.

Richard was now the most powerful man in England after Edward himself, for the discredited Clarence, although forgiven, was never again trusted by his brother. Now was the time for an ambitious man to contract a brilliant alliance with a foreign heiress who might have brought him the prospect of a throne. Instead, Richard asked his brother's consent to his marriage with Anne Neville, the second daughter of Warwick, who had been married to Edward of Lancaster, killed at Tewkesbury. There seems no reason other than affection for such a choice, for Anne was now penniless, Warwick's estates being forfeited to the Crown.[11]

Clarence, in no way deterred by his own record of disloyalty, laid claim to them by right of his wife Isobel. After Tewkesbury, Anne had been sent to the care of her sister, but either to escape Clarence or by his agency she shortly afterwards disappeared. After much searching the Duke of Gloucester discovered her in London disguised as a kitchen maid, and with the utmost propriety conducted her to sanctuary at St Martin's le Grand.

There followed a battle royal between Richard and Clarence which came perilously near to open violence (*Paston Letters*). Clarence was by no means anxious to see his younger brother married to his sister-in-law with the loss of her share of Warwick's estates. Richard, on the other hand, though he could undoubtedly have got anything he wanted in the way of estates from Edward, did not see why his wife should be deprived of her inheritance to please Clarence. Finally an agreement was reached whereby Richard married Anne and received the Yorkshire estates which had been Warwick's, including Middleham, which he always loved beyond all his other castles, while Clarence received the remaining and larger portion of Warwick's property including the earldoms of Warwick and Salisbury.[12] From a worldly point of view Clarence had by far the better part of the bargain, but Richard had Anne and the home he loved, and there is nothing to indicate that he ever regretted it. They were married immediately without waiting for the dispensation which was technically required for the union of cousins, and apparently with little pomp, for no description of the ceremony survives.

Directly afterwards they left London for Middleham, probably with relief, for a court filled with Woodvilles and with George of Clarence can hardly have been attractive to either of them. Anne's mother, the widowed Countess of Warwick, whose claims had been completely disregarded by everyone, was escorted from the sanctuary at Beaulieu by Sir James Tyrell to make her home with her daughter. Richard also interceded for George Neville, Archbishop of York and Warwick's brother, who had been implicated in the recent rebellion, and the following year the Archbishop was released.

Edward gave Richard complete control of England north of the Trent. He was indeed 'Lord of the North', with his own Council at York and power equal to that of the King which he might well have abused as Warwick had, but never did.[13] He set about bringing law and order to that turbulent region which included the Scottish borders, always more or less in turmoil. It was not only the Scots, however, with whom Richard had to contend. The north of England had always been Lancastrian in sympathy, but by his efficiency and justice Richard made himself so personally beloved that popular sentiment became whole heartedly Yorkist, remaining so long after the House of York had come to a bloody end on Bosworth field. He kept up a princely establishment, whenever possible at his favourite Middleham, but also at Pontefract, Carlisle, and other towns which he visited from time to time in the course of his duties. His hospitality was famous, and his genius for administration brought order to a part of the country to which it was something of a novelty.

His only legitimate son, Edward, was born about 1473, a delicate child of a delicate mother. He already had two illegitimate children, a boy and a girl, whom he acknowledged, but from the time of his marriage to Anne Neville he seems to have been a model husband, for no gossip exists about his family life.

In 1475 he accompanied his brother on the expedition to France on the outcome of which he expressed such emphatic disapproval. He probably returned to England a disillusioned man, and the Court saw little of him during the ensuing years. An atmosphere of intrigue was distasteful to him, perhaps because he evidently had no aptitude for it. He contrived to remain on friendly terms with the Queen and her family, principally by keeping out of the way, a course for which his duties in the north gave him ample excuse. After his marriage he lodged when in London at Crosby Place, a splendid house in Bishopsgate which belonged to the widow of a London merchant, Sir John Crosby, but his visits to the capital seem to have been few, and were probably confined to attendances when parliament was sitting. In January 1478 he was present at the marriage of the King's second son, Richard Duke of York, to the heiress of the Mowbrays, Dukes of Norfolk, the bridegroom and bride being four and a half and five years old respectively. A month later Clarence met his mysterious end in the Tower, in spite of Richard's efforts to save his life. He is reported to have blamed the Woodvilles for his brother's death and to have vowed vengeance on the family (*Mancini*).

For many years the difference in character between Edward and Richard had grown more obviously apparent and it is probable that the sympathy between them had correspondingly lessened. Edward always retained the radiant personal charm which endeared him to his subjects even when his physical attractions had degenerated into coarseness and his extravagant court made heavy demands on their pockets. He was an astute politician, a shrewd man of business, and his understanding of the intrigues of his court enabled him to play off one faction against the other and thus keep in check the passions and hatreds of his followers. He had amassed an enormous personal fortune through excursions into trade, principally deals in wool which at that time was England's chief export. He was quite unscrupulous where his profit or his pleasure was concerned, but it appears that there was nothing which his supporters, his subjects, or his Queen would not forgive him.

Richard's personality was much more restrained. He lacked his brother's flamboyance as well as his easy affability. He had to work for the popularity which came so easily to Edward. His gifts were administrative, and his virtues loyalty, courage, and a great sense of justice. It follows that he was no politician. He had no gift for intrigue and no idea of expediency, which he would probably have scorned in any case. The key to his character lies in the personal motto which he chose: 'Loyaulte me lie' – Loyalty binds me. All his life he strove to live up to it and, which finally brought about his downfall, expected others to do the same.

Both brothers were patrons of the arts and of the new learning which was coming into England from across the Channel. Richard was particularly fond of music, and gifted musicians flocked to his household. He was very devout, and the records note many princely gifts to the Church both before and after he became king. He was a generous patron of the Universities of Oxford and Cambridge.

As Edward's reign drew towards its close he left more and more of the administration of his realm to his brother in the north. After the successful expedition against the Scots in 1480 Richard came to London to receive the thanks of parliament and of his brother Edward, who wrote to the Pope himself telling him of the victory and thanking God 'for the support received from our most loving brother'. Richard remained in London over the Christmas of 1482, during which time the news of Louis of France's perfidy reached Edward. On February 20th parliament rose and Richard rode northwards again, bidding Edward farewell, as it turned out, for the last time.

Falcon and Fetterlock

III

LORD PROTECTOR OF ENGLAND

*T*he sudden death of the King was the signal for an outbreak of feverish activity on the part of the Queen and her family. The Woodvilles were well aware that the day the Duke of Gloucester reached London and assumed the Protectorship would see the end of their present power as well as of their hopes for the future. At the moment they seemed to hold all the cards in their hands. They had a firm family nucleus in the Council consisting of Lionel, Bishop of Salisbury, the Marquis Dorset and Sir Edward Woodville, supported by a clerical party which was headed by John Morton, Bishop of Ely. Morton was a man of great ability with a cold, calculating, astute brain who had entered the Church in his youth as a way to personal power and advancement. He had been a firm supporter of Lancaster, following Queen Margaret into exile and returning with her, to be taken prisoner after the battle of Tewkesbury. It is probable that he was always a Lancastrian at heart, in so far as he cared for any cause other than the cause of John Morton, but after Tewkesbury he trimmed his sails so well to the Yorkist wind that he soon found himself in high favour with Edward, who made him Master of the Rolls and recognized the value of his ingenious mind, particularly in matters of intrigue and finance, where scruples, which never troubled Morton, might prove a handicap to the successful prosecution of the business in hand. There is nothing to show what terms he was on with the Duke of Gloucester, but it is hardly likely that the two men had much in common, and on Edward's death he threw in his lot with the Queen.

Besides this useful bloc in the Council the Marquis Dorset was Constable of the Tower which contained not only the Mint but the vast personal treasure amassed by the late King. Most important of all, Lord Rivers and Sir Richard Grey held the person of the twelve-year-old King himself at Ludlow, and the urgent necessity from the Woodville point of view was to get the boy to London and the crown on his head before the Lord Protector could arrive to take a hand in the proceedings.

After a violent altercation in the Council, at which Lord Hastings opposed the Woodville plan to bring Edward to London with a large armed force, it was agreed that his escort should be limited to two thousand men, still a considerable number to guard a king whose title had not yet been in any way questioned. Dorset used half the treasure in the Tower to equip and man a fleet under Sir Edward Woodville for the ostensible reason of defending the coasts against French marauders, though it could be equally well used for less innocent ends. The remainder of the treasure Dorset divided between himself and his mother. Letters were dispatched to Rivers impressing on him the need for bringing the young King to London by May 1st, the coronation being fixed for the 4th. No official letters appear to have been dispatched to the Lord Protector telling him of his brother's death.

Patents were issued to persons appointed to collect taxes in the names of Dorset and Rivers, with no mention of the Duke of Gloucester, and his name was also omitted from the bidding prayer written for the convocation of bishops, the persons mentioned being 'our dread lord King Edward V; the lady Queen Elizabeth; all the royal children; his nobles and people' – wording which places Elizabeth Woodville in the position of a Queen Regent and which makes the omission of the Lord Protector rather more than pointed. So certain was Dorset that nothing could interfere with their plans that he boasted 'We are so important that even without the King's uncle we can make and enforce our decisions' (*Mancini*).

In spite of Dorset's confidence there was much uneasiness among the more moderate members of the Council, uneasiness which spread to the general public. People remembered the disasters which had resulted from the minorities of Richard II and Henry VI, and few were anxious to see a third, dominated by the hated Woodvilles. London was a city full of doubts and fears.

News of the late King's death reached Ludlow about the middle of the month and at the same time the Duke of Buckingham, who was on his Welsh estates, also received the tidings. Richard's whereabouts at the time are uncertain; he may have been at Middleham, though some historians say he was away inspecting the fortifications on the Scottish border. It is probable that he did not hear the news of his brother's death until some ten days after it happened, and then it was in letters from Lord Hastings which could have told him little but the bare fact and his own appointment as Lord Protector.

Richard wrote letters of condolence to the Queen, and also one to the Council, in which he expressed his willingness to undertake his brother's charge (*Mancini*). He then set out for London immediately, but with no undue haste. He did not take an armed force with him, but an escort of six hundred gentlemen of the north, all in mourning. He stopped at York where he caused requiem masses to be said for his brother and led the local magnates in taking a solemn oath of allegiance to his nephew. In the midst of these pious observances he received a further letter from Lord Hastings telling him of developments in London, and leaving him in little doubt that there was no time to be lost if the young King was to be crowned without the almost certain risk of civil strife. At the same time he received letters from the Duke of Buckingham, offering him his support, to which he returned an answer asking the Duke to meet him at Northampton.[14]

Richard left York, still with no more than his 'mourning train', and arrived at Northampton on April 29th. Here he found Rivers with the news that the King had gone on to Stony Stratford without waiting to greet his uncle and guardian. Stony Stratford was fourteen miles nearer London, a fact which undoubtedly did not escape the Duke of Gloucester. He entertained Rivers at his inn, being joined during the evening by the Duke of Buckingham, who had brought with him an escort of three hundred men. When Rivers retired for the night the two Dukes, both of royal blood, held a conference at which the latest news from London was discussed, and disturbing enough it must have been. Buckingham, who, married to one of the Queen's sisters, was unwavering in his hatred of the Woodvilles and who had spent far more time at Court during the past years than Richard had, probably opened the Protector's eyes to much that he had previously underrated. Whether it was Hastings' news or Buckingham's revelations or some other source of which we know nothing that made him act, Richard took swift steps next morning to deal with the ugly situation which was developing. He arrested Rivers and rode on to Stony Stratford, where he found the young King about to leave for London. Although his escort combined with Buckingham's fell short by eleven hundred men and baggage wagons full of weapons of the force which was accompanying the King, he arrested Richard Grey and two members of the King's household, Sir Richard Haute and Sir Thomas Vaughan, and sent them, with Rivers, back to detention in the north. Grey was sent to Middleham and Rivers to Sheriff Hutton, while the King's escort was dismissed.

This done he proceeded to London with his nephew and Buckingham, having dealt neatly with a situation which might well have ended in considerable bloodshed.

The news of the happenings at Northampton and Stony Stratford had preceded the royal party. London was in an uproar, seething with rumours and anxiety. The Queen, after trying without success to raise a force to resist the Lord Protector (*Mancini*), fled to sanctuary at Westminster, taking with her her five daughters, her younger son Richard Duke of York, and all the valuables she could lay her hands on. In fact the sanctuary wall had to be breached to admit the bulkier goods. Thomas Rotherham, Archbishop of York and Keeper of the Great Seal, in a panic and quite unconstitutionally, delivered the Seal to the Queen in the middle of the night, though next morning he recovered his nerve and retrieved it. Dorset went into hiding and at the earliest opportunity took ship for France. The Woodvilles' brief dream of supreme power was for the time being over, but it was into an unhappy and restless city that the Lord Protector escorted his nephew on May 4th, presenting him to the people who lined the route as their King. Young Edward went to the palace of the Bishop of London, and the Duke of Gloucester to his mother's house, Baynard's Castle.

Richard lost no time in taking control of the situation, and the ordinary machinery of government began to function once more. His position as Lord Protector was ratified by the Council, and preparations for the coronation of Edward were immediately put in hand, the date being fixed for June 22nd. Grants and proclamations were issued in the name of the young King, who on May 19th moved his residence to the Tower in conformity with the usual practice of his ancestors, who had been accustomed to spend the weeks before their coronation in that fortress which was also the principal royal palace.

Richard had no forces in the city beyond his own personal escort and he made no attempt to summon reinforcements from the north, though on June 5th the Duchess of Gloucester joined him at Crosby Place. The Duke of Buckingham had a considerable establishment in London, as had also Lord Hastings, Lord Stanley, and other great nobles, but for six weeks the life of the city, the carrying on of the government, and preparations for the coronation continued in normal fashion. John Russell, Bishop of Lincoln, made a draft of the speech which, as Lord Chancellor in place of the excitable Rotherham, he would deliver at the opening of parliament.

It was on June 9th that a sudden change came over the scene. On that day the Council met at Westminster. There is no record of what transpired, but it is evident that a further plot by the Woodvilles came to light, for on June 10th Richard wrote urgently to the city of York for reinforcements against 'the Queen her blood adherents and affinity which have intended and daily doth intend to murder and utterly destroy us and our cousin the Duke of Buckingham and the old royal blood of this realm' (*York Civic Records, Davies*).

Only a few days before, Richard had written an ordinary routine letter to York on local matters about which the city fathers were concerned; a letter which contained no suggestion of urgency or need for assistance. Evidently whatever had happened was both serious and unexpected. Sir Richard Ratcliffe, who carried the second letter to York, bore a similar appeal for help to Lord Neville, as well as orders that Rivers, Grey, Haute, and Vaughan should be tried immediately for high treason.[15]

Three days later, on June 13th, the famous Council meeting was held in the Tower. There is only one account of this, that attributed to Sir Thomas More, which will be fully examined later in this book. It is sufficient to say here that Richard suddenly accused his old friend Hastings, together with Morton, Stanley, and Rotherham, of plotting with the Queen and Jane Shore against his authority and his life. Hastings was ordered to be executed immediately, Stanley was imprisoned but released almost immediately, while Morton was committed to the custody of the Duke of Buckingham. Jane Shore was arrested and handed over to the Church, which condemned her to do penance as a harlot and to lose her possessions. On the whole the fair Jane got off very lightly and was by no means at the end of her resources, for this is not the last we hear of her.

On June 16th the Archbishop of Canterbury persuaded Elizabeth Woodville to allow her younger son to leave sanctuary and join his brother in the Tower. The coronation was postponed till November. On June 22nd a sermon was preached at St Paul's Cross in which the preacher, Dr Shaw, revealed to the world the secret which was probably the subject of the Council's anxious meeting on the 9th. He is believed to have announced that the children of Edward IV by Elizabeth Woodville were illegitimate because at the time of that secret ceremony at Grafton Edward was already contracted to the Lady Eleanor Butler, widow of Sir Thomas Butler and daughter of the first Earl of Shrewsbury. Dr Shaw is by some chroniclers reputed to have impugned the legitimacy of Edward IV himself, but this seems highly unlikely, for Richard was then, and remained, on the best of terms with his mother, which is hardly compatible with his allowing her to be publicly slandered. The authority for Edward's bigamy was Robert Stillington, Bishop of Bath and Wells, who claimed to have married the King to Lady Eleanor. He is said to have produced good and sufficient proofs of his story which have not survived, though they were accepted at the time and subsequently embodied in an act of parliament. Stillington himself had been in high favour with Edward, until at the time of the death of Clarence he had been suddenly sent to the Tower on a vague charge of speaking words to the detriment of the King, and was only released on giving a solemn promise that he would not repeat his offence. Some similar charge was one of those brought against Clarence himself, who may have learnt something from Stillington which constituted a danger to Edward's children.

The story is in all probability true; it is in keeping with Edward's character where women were concerned, and there is a curious reference to a letter written by his mother at the time of his marriage to Elizabeth Woodville in which the Duchess of York implores her son not to commit the sin of bigamy (*More*).[16] On the other hand, it may have been invented or at least welcomed by members of the Council who, frightened by recent events, wished to avoid the dangers attendant on a minority inflamed by the plots of the boy-King's maternal relations. There is no final proof either way, but Richard's behaviour up to the middle of June is inconsistent with his having any knowledge of the story, true or false. His actions are those of a man who has been committed to a certain course of action and whose plans are suddenly and violently upset.

On June 25th a gathering took place at Westminster which was a parliament in all but legal name, consisting of the peers summoned to attend what would have been Edward's first parliament, most of the commons, and reinforced by the leading citizens of London. The Lord Protector's claim to the throne was examined in the light of the proofs of the Butler marriage produced by Stillington. A petition was drawn up asking him to accept the Crown with the unanimous approval of the gathering.

The following day a deputation waited on Richard at his mother's house and, the Duke of Buckingham acting as its spokesman, presented the petition with an eloquent plea that he should accept so that the country might escape the dangers of a disputed title and a minority, and enjoy peace and firm government under a man whose birth could not be impugned. In any case, he said, they would not have the sons of Edward IV to reign over them, and if the Lord Protector refused they would choose someone else. With an appearance of considerable reluctance Richard accepted. His reluctance was probably genuine but, whatever his motives, he undoubtedly averted a renewal of civil war by his acceptance. His brother had left him two trusts, his country and his children, but Edward had also left him a situation which made it utterly impossible for him to fulfil them both.

Livery Collar of Edward IV

IV

TREASON

R ichard was crowned with his Queen on July 6th at a ceremony which was graced by almost the whole peerage, both Yorkist and Lancastrian. The common people, who had not unnaturally received the startling events of the past three weeks with caution, seem to have accepted the outcome with equanimity, for there is no record of any disturbance having marred the harmony of the proceedings. The men from York arrived a week before the coronation; far from being picked troops summoned to assist a long-planned usurpation they were obviously hastily raised levies whose shabby equipment was a source of merriment to the Londoners. On their way south they had assisted at Pontefract at the execution of Rivers, Grey, Haute, and Vaughan, who had been tried before the Earl of Northumberland and condemned for treason.[17] Elizabeth Woodville's plottings had lost her brother and son their heads, her other son his crown, and reduced herself from the position of Queen of England to that of Dame Elizabeth Grey, mistress of the late King.

Richard's first action on his accession was to take his seat on the King's Bench in Westminster Hall and from there to deliver a strict injunction to the Justices and Serjeants at Law, before a vast gathering, that they should administer justice impartially to all his subjects. His actions showed that he was determined to justify his acceptance of the crown by the exercise of mercy and justice. Unfortunately he had to deal with too many who did not know the meaning of either word.

Dominic Mancini gives an interesting contemporary account of the rumours current in London in the weeks preceding Richard's accession. Mancini was an Italian priest who had spent about a year in England, leaving the country immediately after Richard's coronation to return to France, where he wrote down his impressions for the benefit of his patron, Angelo Cato, Archbishop of Vienne.

He expresses his reluctance to put on paper these impressions, admitting that he 'had not sufficiently ascertained . . . the secret designs of men in this whole affair'.

He relates the gossip of the day, and from his narrative it is easy to understand Richard's reluctance to accept the crown under such circumstances.

The King can have had no delusions as to the difficulties which confronted him, or the mischief which could be made out of the manner of his accession. London was full of dangerous undercurrents beneath the surface of rejoicing. The upheavals of the past weeks had given rise to a great deal of gossip, much of it ingenuous and the outcome of a natural, if sentimental, sympathy for the young Edward, but there was also a great number of rumours which were more venomous, and inspired by the supporters of the Woodvilles who, if their plots had failed, still had tongues which they used. Whispers went round that the lives of Edward IV's sons were in danger; these rumours were encouraged both by the Woodville bloc and by those who still secretly favoured the House of Lancaster, and began to revive the hopes so precariously based on the slender claim of Henry Tudor. Elizabeth Woodville was still in sanctuary at Westminster with her five daughters while her two sons were lodged in the royal palace of the Tower two miles away.

With this explosive situation in the capital the newly crowned King made the grave mistake of setting out on a progress to his beloved north country a fortnight after his coronation. Sick of intrigue and impatient to breathe again the more congenial air of the north, where also his son was waiting for him, he did not stay to consolidate his position in London, or to deal with the dangerous elements which threatened it. He left his capital to make his way north through Reading, Oxford, the Cotswolds, Gloucester, Warwick, and Leicester to York. At Gloucester the Duke of Buckingham, who had taken such a prominent part in the events which raised his cousin Richard to the throne, left the royal train and rode to his castle of Brecknock, where he enjoyed the interesting society of his prisoner John Morton.

The progress was a triumphant success. The King was greeted everywhere with enthusiasm by high and low alike. The Bishop of St David's, Dr Thomas Langton, writing to the Prior of Christ

Church, says that '. . . the King . . . contents the people where he goes best that ever did prince, for many a poor man that hath suffered wrong many days hath been relieved and helped by him and his commands in his progress. And in many great cities and towns were great sums of money given him which he hath refused. On my truth I liked never the conditions of any prince so well as his. God hath sent him to us for the weal of us all.' (*Christ Church Letters*).

York welcomed its lord with delight and gorgeous ceremonies, at one of which Richard knighted his little son Edward, not yet ten years old.[18] In the middle of September he turned south again, and as the walls of the city faded out of sight, so faded the glowing hopes of his reign. When he reached Lincoln the news reached him that the south was about to rise in rebellion, and that the leader of the rebellion was none other than his trusted supporter the Duke of Buckingham.

Nobody has ever been able to explain Buckingham's astounding change of allegiance. Traitor, knave, and fool, he was all three, but the reason for showing his true colours within three months of assisting with such apparent enthusiasm at the coronation of his cousin who had treated him with the utmost generosity, remains a mystery. The rebellion had been launched with gatherings of people whose sympathy drove them to demand the removal of the ex-King and the Duke of York from the Tower. Soon, however, the rumours changed and stories 'were spread' (*Croyland Chronicle*) that the children had already been murdered, while the object of the disturbances was quietly changed to a scheme to bring Henry Tudor over from Brittany, set him on the throne and marry him to Elizabeth of York, the eldest daughter of Edward IV and Elizabeth Woodville. The prime movers in this plot were the Duke of Buckingham, his supposed prisoner John Morton, Bishop of Ely, and Margaret Beaufort, mother of Henry Tudor, now married to Lord Stanley.

Buckingham's father and grandfather had both died fighting for the Lancastrians and it has been suggested that Buckingham himself had always been a Lancastrian at heart and had been working all the time for a Lancastrian restoration (*Carte*). Morton was primarily interested in his own advancement and could see a rosy future for himself as the chief adviser during a Woodville minority, but none at all with Richard of Gloucester on the throne. When the Woodville hopes came to an abrupt end he returned to his old allegiance, with Henry Tudor as Lancaster's heir. As it eventually turned out he could not have found a more congenial master. Lady Stanley's motive was simple: the throne of England for her only son.

However, on this occasion the revolt met with no success. His own incompetence, combined with floods which prevented him from crossing the Severn, proved the downfall of Buckingham. He was captured, tried for high treason at Salisbury and executed, as he deserved. Lady Stanley's life was spared on condition that her husband should be responsible for her good behaviour.[19] Morton escaped to join Henry Tudor. Richard showed great leniency towards the rebels; there were few executions and he restored many forfeited estates to their dependants. The rumours about the two boys died down in England, though they persisted on the continent where they had probably been hatched.

In January 1483/4 Richard held his first and only parliament, which passed laws that forced Bacon, in an otherwise adverse criticism of Richard, to admit that he was 'a good law-maker for the ease and solace of the common people' (*Life of Henry VII*). These measures included the right to bail and the redressing of certain abuses which had crept into the system of land tenure. The qualifications for jury service were tightened up and the dangerous practices of maintenance and livery were declared illegal, as was Edward IV's favourite system of money raising, the 'benevolence'. These reforms benefited Richard's humbler subjects, but they were not popular with the nobles and the official classes whose interests suffered, and they lost Richard much support which he was to need badly later on.

To Richard himself the most important act passed by this parliament was that known as the *Titulus Regius*, which set out at length, and endorsed, the petition by which Richard had been offered the crown in the previous June. Richard's title and that of his heirs had now received the full authority of the statute book.

In February 1483/4 Elizabeth Woodville left sanctuary and with her daughters placed herself under Richard's protection, while he made a solemn promise before his Council that he would respect their persons and provide suitably for their futures as his kinswomen. That Elizabeth should require such a promise is not surprising, considering her own activities during the past year and her schemings with Margaret Beaufort, Lady Stanley, and Henry Tudor. At a later date Elizabeth wrote to her son Dorset in France telling him to return to England where the King 'would treat him well'. Dorset set out to obey her instructions but was forcibly prevented from leaving France by Henry's adherents (*Polydore Vergil*).

In April 1484 Richard sustained a devastating, and indeed fatal, blow in the sudden death at Middleham of his only son, Edward Prince of Wales. The significance of this loss cannot be over-estimated. Richard appears to have been a devoted father and all his personal hopes had been centred on this boy, but beyond this the future of his dynasty and the assured succession of his line, so essential to the peace of the country and the stability of his throne, died with the child, while the Queen's delicate health made it impossible that she should give her husband other children. Thus the country was faced once more with the hazards of a disputed succession, and with the memory of a hundred years of civil war for this same cause behind them the people had some reason for renewed misgivings. Richard himself did not become less popular, but the prospect of a childless King certainly undermined his subjects' faith in the future.

The death of the Prince of Wales was followed by another outbreak of rumours concerning the fate of the sons of Edward IV, for the idea of immediate retribution was very firmly fixed in the mediaeval mind. As before, the rumours seem to have come from across the Channel, where they had been publicly referred to by the French Chancellor in January. Henry Tudor once more saw opportunity open before him as the result of Richard's loss. He had sworn to marry Elizabeth, the undoubted daughter of Edward IV whether legitimate or not, and so to unite the Lancastrian and Yorkist factions. He was thus the potential progenitor of a dynasty which under the circumstances might well have an appeal to Richard's anxious subjects, whose chief wish was for peace in an assured future. There was much coming and going of Henry's agents and the rumours grew and multiplied.

In March 1485 the Queen died. Richard is said to have wept openly at her funeral, but more rumours were immediately started to the effect that he had poisoned her in order to marry his niece Elizabeth. Richard was obliged to issue a public denial of this story, which had given great offence to many of his subjects. How his position could ever have been improved by marrying his brother's illegitimate daughter is difficult to see, and there is reason to believe that he was proposing to marry her to the Earl of Desmond (*BL. Harl. MS. 433*), but it was another fine piece of mud to fling at the unfortunate King.

Several of the disgruntled nobles began a treasonable correspondence with Henry, chief among them being his step-father Lord Stanley and his step-uncle Sir William Stanley. Richard, ever slow to recognize treachery among those he believed to be his friends, was long in ignorance of the treason with which he was surrounded, though by now it was recognized that Henry would make a bid for the throne. Richard even made Lord Stanley and his son Lord Strange Commissioners of Array in Wales and the Welsh marches, while Northumberland was all powerful in the north.

Throughout his reign Richard had been pressed for money, the Woodvilles having made away with the late King's fortune, and Richard himself having been extremely open-handed in rewarding his friends and in many cases remitting the property forfeited by his enemies to their relatives. Now that the realm was threatened with invasion he found it necessary to raise money for its defence. He did not, however, resort to Edward's hated benevolences, which his own parliament had declared illegal. He sent messages to the wealthier among his subjects asking for loans for which he gave security and the promise of repayment at specified dates (*BL. Harl. MS. 433*). With the money thus raised he equipped an army and took up his headquarters at Nottingham.

Henry landed at Milford Haven in August 1485 with a force composed of foreign mercenaries and the remnants of the Lancastrian party, and paid for with money provided by his mother Lady Stanley and the French. Sir William Stanley openly supported the rebels and was proclaimed a traitor. Lord Stanley, while still professing loyalty to Richard, secretly promised his support to his step-son. The two armies met near Market Bosworth in Leicestershire on August 22nd. The battle lasted barely two hours, Sir William Stanley throwing his force into the fight on Henry's side, while Northumberland, who commanded the King's rear, and Lord Stanley took no part in the proceedings at all.

Richard, seeing himself betrayed on all sides, made a desperate bid to retrieve the day, charging at the head of a small band of faithful friends into the heart of the enemy ranks, where he was killed, fighting bravely in the midst of his enemies. His last cry was that of 'Treason! Treason!'

After the battle his body was found under a heap of dead, and was taken back to Leicester, stripped naked and thrown across the back of a pack horse. There it was exposed to the insults of the mob for two days, after which he was buried by the charity of the monks in the church of the Grey Friars.

Richard was deeply mourned, particularly in the north where he was best known. There is no truth in the story that the people turned against him; his downfall was brought about by a combination of adverse circumstances, the disloyalty of three discontented nobles, and one scheming woman. Entirely loyal himself, he was unable to recognize treachery in others or to deal with it with sufficient ruthlessness when it became obvious. His leniency towards traitors was both remarkable and fatal; it cost him his crown, his life, and his reputation.

Rose-en-Soleil

THE LEGEND

V

THE USURPER

*T*he royal circlet which Richard had worn round his helmet during the battle of Bosworth was found in a thorn bush on the field, and with a perfect sense of drama Lord Stanley placed it on his step-son's head amid the acclamations of his followers. This unknown Welshman, who had come from overseas and with the help of foreign mercenaries and a few English traitors had picked the Crown of England out of a bramble thicket on a Leicestershire hillside, was well aware that his difficulties were only beginning.

The House of York had ruled England for twenty-five years with one short break in 1470 and it was on the whole immensely popular, in spite of the feud between the Woodville faction and the old aristocracy which had come to a head over the question of Edward IV's successor. The people had then been content to accept the rule of a grown man of undisputed birth and ability rather than that of a child of doubtful legitimacy who could not fail to be the centre of a struggle for power.

Henry Tudor on the contrary was not known at all in England, having fled the country after Tewkesbury at the age of fifteen. His support came from the scattered remnants of the Lancastrian party to which was added the Woodville following and the Stanleys. He would have received no support from the Yorkists had he not promised to marry the Lady Elizabeth, eldest daughter of Edward IV.[20] This necessity was deeply distasteful to Henry, who had no wish to reign in right of his wife, and he showed little anxiety to hurry on the marriage, which only took place in January 1485/6 after he himself had been crowned alone, and after he had been subjected to considerable pressure from his followers. Even so it was two years before he could bring himself to allow the coronation of his Queen to take place, a delay which caused great discontent among his subjects.

At the time of Bosworth, Henry was a young man in his twenty-ninth year. He had spent the preceding fifteen years as an exile at foreign courts, always in danger and the centre of intrigue. He was of a deeply suspicious nature with a subtle tortuous mind which delighted in secrecy. He was cold, calculating, ruthless and quite unscrupulous.

This was the man who was faced with the difficult task of consolidating a victory which treachery had given him, and a position to which he had no right. He had to discredit the house of York while relying on its popularity in the person of his intended bride to bolster up his non-existent claim, and he had to do it without appearing to assume the crown in her right. It was therefore essential that the invasion of England, the killing of her lawful, elected, and crowned King and the usurpation of his throne should have some moral justification, so that it should not appear what it was, a piece of highly successful buccaneering.

Henry, whose own mind was subtle and far-seeing and who had, since the failure of Buckingham's rebellion, had the advantage of John Morton's constant and valuable advice, had been preparing the ground for the past two years. Morton was now irretrievably committed to the fortunes of the Tudors. All his hopes and ambitions for the future lay in the success of Henry's cause, besides which master and counsellor found in each the complement of the other. There can seldom have been a more congenial partnership, for both preferred hidden and tortuous methods to direct action as a means to their ends, and both fully understood the advantages of calumny and insinuation as weapons of policy. The whispering campaign which they had conducted against Richard was one which they could plan with that relish which puts a fine edge on achievement.

Henry's agents had been busy throughout England spreading stories detrimental to the King for months before Bosworth. William Colyngbourne, the man who pinned the famous distich:

> The Cat, the Rat and Lovell our dog
> Rule all England under the Hog

on the door of St Paul's, and was executed for 'treasonable correspondence with Henry Tydder' was one of these. Richard had been accused – anonymously – of infanticide, regicide, immoral designs on his niece, and even of murdering his wife. That the stories never attained a higher status than that of common gossip is proof in itself that they received little credence, though they were doubtless repeated with fearful relish among the ignorant.[21]

Now Richard was dead, slain by the treason of false friends, and the treatment which his dead body received after Bosworth was but another step in the carefully planned campaign of denigration. His corpse was treated as carrion, as that of a creature whose wickedness had placed him outside the pale of human decency, of a monster from whom Henry had risked his life to deliver the people of England. Not only was Richard himself thus presented to his former subjects as something beneath contempt, but the whole dynasty of York was dishonoured in the person of the last Yorkist king. Henry could not attack the father of his future wife, but the dead Richard could be used to serve political expediency as well as Henry's personal dislike of York, so that the Tudor dynasty might yet flourish on a Yorkist dung-heap.

Henry was crowned at Westminster in October and immediately afterwards held his first parliament. It was faced with the initial difficulty of finding him a title to the throne which would present some semblance of legality since, placed on the statute book less than two years before, was the *Titulus Regius*, which set down as clearly as words could define it the undoubted right of Richard Plantagenet, together with all the circumstances which had led to his acceptance of the crown, the whole being 'said, affirmed, signified, and remembered in a full parliament and by the authority of the same attested and approved' *(Rolls. Parl. I Ric. III)*.

Here was the proof in black and white that Richard being no usurper, Henry was. Henry's obvious course was to have the whole question of the legitimacy or otherwise of Edward's children re-opened and to disprove the pre-contract with Lady Eleanor Butler – if he could. He did nothing of the kind. Instead he repealed the Act *unread*, giving orders that it should be deleted from the statute book and that all copies should be destroyed under pain of heavy punishment 'so that all things said and remembered in the said Bill and Act thereof may be for ever out of remembrance and also forgot.' *(Rolls. Parl. I Hen. VII)*. We owe our knowledge of this important Act to the fact that the original draft was overlooked in the general destruction, and only came to light in the seventeenth century among a mass of documents in the Tower, while at about the same time its gist was found in the manuscript of the contemporary *Chronicle of Croyland*, a remote monastery buried in the fen country of Lincolnshire.²² There is only one reasonable explanation for Henry's arbitrary decree: he was unable to disprove the pre-contract, which had existed, thus making Richard's claim to the throne good and himself a rebel and usurper.

Having disposed of the awkward *Titulus Regius* Henry's parliament proceeded to the attainder of Richard and his adherents. In this again it was confronted with a difficulty, for there was no doubt whatever that Richard had been crowned and annointed King of England and in law it was impossible to attaint him or his loyal followers of treason. Henry got over this obstacle by dating his own reign from the *day before Bosworth*. This bland assumption gave rise to considerable disagreement even in his packed parliament, but the Act was finally passed because 'it was the King's pleasure' (*Bacon*). It is worth quoting:

> Wherefore our sovereign Lord, calling unto his blessed remembrance this high charge adjoined to his royal majesty and estate, nor oblivious or putting out of his godly mind the unnatural mischievous and great perjuries, treasons, homicides, and murders in shedding of infant's blood, with many other wrongs, odious offences and abominations against God and man, and in especial our said sovereign Lord, committed and done by Richard late Duke of Gloucester, calling and naming himself by usurpation King Richard III, the which with John Duke of Norfolk, Thomas Earl of Surrey etc, etc., . . . the 21st day of August the first year of our sovereign lord assembled to them at Leicester . . . a great host traitorously intending, imagining and conspiring the destruction of the King's royal person, our sovereign liege Lord. And they . . . by great and continued deliberation traitorously levied war against our sovereign Lord and his true subjects [*Rolls. Parl. I Hen. VII*].

While highly imaginative over matters of known fact, the Act is remarkably reticent in other respects. During the past two years Henry's agents had been busily occupied in spreading rumours to the effect that Richard had had his two nephews murdered in the Tower, and in later years Tudor historians tell us that it was this abominable deed which turned the country against him and caused it to welcome Henry as a deliverer. By the repeal of the *Titulus Regius* Henry had legitimized all the children of Edward IV. He was about to marry one of them, but the repeal had also replaced Edward's two sons in the succession before their sister and very much before Henry himself.

It was therefore doubly important that he should re-assert the death of the boys. By so doing he would endorse his policy of blackening his late rival's name with the full force of parliamentary backing, and at the same time he would establish that the direct male line of Edward IV was extinct. It is incredible that with these two compelling motives Henry should have refrained from a direct and damning accusation against Richard, followed by a hue and cry after the actual murderers so that they might be brought to public trial. However, the charges are the conventional ones which appear repeatedly in acts of attainder, tyranny, 'shedding of infants' blood', and so on, and no steps appear to have been taken to find the instruments of the crime and to extract confessions from them.[23] Had Henry known the boys to be dead from whatever cause, nothing would have been easier than to invent the necessary evidence which would have finally damned Richard throughout the civilized world, and would have saved Henry himself from the succession of claimants which shortly began to appear. There can only be one explanation of this extraordinary failure to seize a superb opportunity on the part of a man who was accustomed to make the most of opportunities; the children had not been murdered at all, and one at least of them was still alive. Either they were in Henry's hands and a great embarrassment to him or else they had been removed to a place of safety, unknown or out of Henry's reach, in which case he would not dare to insist on their death, knowing that at any moment they might be produced to give him the lie. It is very significant that there is no record of any requiem mass having been ordered for the children who, if they had died violent deaths, would have stood in particular need of spiritual assistance.[24] Such a ceremony would have been of the greatest value to Henry as a means of emphasizing their deaths, but it would have been a deadly insult to the Church if he had ordered it while knowing them to be alive.[25]

Henry's failure to make any formal announcement or accusation concerning the fate of Edward IV's sons soon produced repercussions. On the occasion of his marriage to Elizabeth the rejoicings of the people were so exuberant as to cause him considerable annoyance at this evidence of the popularity of the house of York. Shortly afterwards he was obliged to hurry to the north, where Richard's personal popularity made his supercessor particularly hated. It must have been galling for St George to realize that the dragon was infinitely preferred to himself.

In September 1486 Henry's Queen bore him a son at Winchester. Her mother Elizabeth Woodville, restored to her royal rank and possessions, was present at the birth and stood godmother to the baby prince. Elizabeth Woodville had now attained her ambition; her daughter was Queen of England and her grandson heir to the throne. Her subsequent behaviour therefore becomes almost inexplicable.

In January 1486/7 news reached Henry from Ireland that a pretender to the throne had appeared. He first claimed to be Richard, Duke of York, the younger of the sons of Edward IV, but almost immediately changed his identity, claiming to be the Earl of Warwick, son of Clarence, who, barred from the succession by his father's attainder, had been treated with great kindness by Richard but, being the only known surviving male Plantagenet, had been imprisoned in the Tower by Henry. The pretender, Lambert Simnel, was a palpable impostor. He was the son of an Oxford tradesman who under the guidance of a priest named Simonds put forward his astonishing claim, which was backed by a number of prominent people who must have very well known it to be false. Among these were Richard III's nephew and heir the Earl of Lincoln, his great friend Lord Lovell, both survivors from Bosworth, his sister Margaret of Burgundy,[26] and, incredibly, *Elizabeth Woodville*. An army was raised to invade England and Simnel was crowned king in Dublin. Henry took the threat of this rebellion very seriously; a Council was immediately called at Sheen to take steps to counter it and one of its acts was to strip Elizabeth of all her possessions and to incarcerate her in the abbey of Bermondsey where she spent the rest of her life in poverty and solitude.[27]

Henry's army met the invaders at Stoke and utterly defeated them. All the leaders were killed including the Earl of Lincoln, and the slaughter among the Irish troops was enormous. This abortive rising was in itself of small importance but its implications are of the greatest interest, for it is evident that Simnel was put up as a cover for someone else. His own claim was from the first an obvious and impudent imposture, yet Margaret of Burgundy, fiercely devoted to her father's house, had given him her assistance, as had the Earl of Lincoln. Henry expressed great regret at the death of the latter, saying that he had hoped to learn from him what lay behind the enterprise. Most astonishing of all is Elizabeth Woodville's participation, for she stood to lose everything both for herself and her daughter.[28] She certainly did not take such risks for the sake of the son of Clarence, the man she had hated and for whose death she had been more than a little responsible. Henry's public excuse for her incarceration was that three years earlier she had made her peace with Richard, an explanation which caused more wondering than her disgrace, as it was generally felt with reason that this offence had long ago been forgiven, and that to rake it up now could only be as a cover for other and more recent offences which the Act condemning her refers to as 'various considerations' (*Bacon*).

Of the facts there seems to be only one explanation which could account for her risking her own future and that of her daughter and grandson: she knew that one of her sons was alive, and the reality behind the imposture of Lambert Simnel. Ambition had been the ruling passion of Elizabeth Woodville's life – ambition for her family, for her children, and above all for herself. Her efforts to gratify this lust for power had led her to intrigue against the Lord Protector, with the result that the country had been brought to the verge of civil war and the crown had been lost to her son. By a strange twist of fortune she had found herself the mother of the Queen consort, an honourable position certainly, but one which carried no influence with her son-in-law. Personal power still eluded her, but if her son could displace the usurper and she herself be the mother of the King regnant instead merely of the Queen consort – that indeed would be a stake worth playing for, though she had recovered so much of her former dignity that she must have been very sure of her son's survival to induce her to take such a risk. The fact that she did take it is in itself sufficient proof that he was alive and that she had sure knowledge of his existence. There could not be a clearer indication that one at least of the boys survived their uncle, Richard.

The suppression of Lambert Simnel's rising brought small comfort to Henry. Even his wife's popularity and the birth of an heir had not brought him the security he had hoped for. Bacon tells us that 'he was not without much hatred throughout the realm. The root of it all was the discountenancing of the house of York which the general body of the realm still affected.' Henry's hatred of his wife's family grew daily. Bacon, in a masterpiece of under-statement, says that he had 'a settled disposition to depress all eminent persons of the House of York'. This disposition, which he left as a dying trust to his son Henry VIII, took the form of depriving the surviving members of that unlucky family of their lives as and when the opportunity presented itself. The first to go was Richard's illegitimate son, John of Gloucester, whom Henry had at first treated with some generosity, giving him a pension of £20 a year. Now, filled with apprehension for the future of his new dynasty, Henry had the young man put away on suspicion of carrying on a correspondence with Ireland. He was the first victim of the series of judicial murders by which the Tudors rid themselves of their rivals and systematically wiped out a whole family over a period of years with a callous ruthlessness which is blood-curdling.

A further source of anxiety to Henry was the continued popu-larity of Richard himself. From his dishonoured grave at Leicester the dead King still exercised a hold on the affections of the people, particularly in the north. It became more and more necessary for the Tudor to discredit Richard's memory and in this congenial task inclination as well as policy urged Henry to renewed efforts. Having been unable to bring a definite charge of murder and regicide against Richard with the authority of parliament, he was obliged to fall back on other means. Probably the hint dropped in the Act of Attainder and a slow and patient policy of denigration spread over the years had more appeal to Henry's devious mind. The campaign of slander against Richard's memory became increasingly virulent, and developed into one of the finest examples of successful propaganda in recorded history. Much of the credit, if that is the word, must go to John Morton, late Bishop of Ely and now Archbishop of Canterbury and Henry's Chancellor, than whom no finer propa-gandist has ever lived. Between them he and the King built a legend on the flimsiest foundations which has lasted five hundred years and has not been discarded yet.[29]

From the first, circumstances were on their side. Nearly all Richard's close friends had died with him at Bosworth; the remnant, like Lincoln and Lovell, had been killed at Stoke. There was nobody of any importance left in a position to defend the late King's memory or to contradict anything that Henry might choose to say about him. Also, conditions in the country were perfect for spreading fantastic stories with the certainty that within a very short time they would come to be accepted as truth, while those who could contradict them would not dare to do so. England had been in a state of intermittent ferment for thirty years, for the most part the people were ignorant and illiterate, communications difficult, and small communities up and down the land virtually isolated. Rumour could not have had a better soil in which to grow.

Printing was in its infancy and books were rare treasures for such as could read them. The art was dependent on the patronage and goodwill of the reigning monarch and if Master Caxton wished to retain the royal favour he was well advised to refrain from printing anything in praise of the late King. It was probably all he could do to live down the eulogy of Richard which had been published at Christmas 1484 in the preface of his book *The Order of Chivalry*. For the next hundred years the printing press was to be a bitter enemy to Richard's memory, and not the printing press alone; it was quite remarkable how the views of men of letters changed almost overnight after Henry's usurpation.

Livery Collar of Richard III

VI

BIRTH OF A LEGEND

*T*here was a chantry priest named Rous who had lived for many years at Guy's Cliff near Warwick. He was an antiquary and a talented artist who had been occupied for some time on a descriptive illustrated history of the Earls of Warwick. This is known today as the *Warwick Roll* and Rous made two copies of it, one in Latin and one in English.[30] The English copy had left his hands before Richard's death. In it the King appears as the husband of Anne Neville, wearing the royal crown and being described as 'a mighty prince and especial good lord' and again as 'the most victorious prince Richard III; in his realm full commendably punishing offenders of the laws, especially oppressors of his commons, and cherishing those that were virtuous, by the which discreet guiding he got great thanks and love of all his subjects rich and poor, and great laud of the people of all other lands about him.' Queen Anne is depicted wearing her crown and royal insignia and their young son the Prince of Wales wears a prince's coronet. This copy remains to this day unaltered as it left Rous' hands, and is now in the British Museum.

The other copy was still in his possession when disaster overtook Richard at Bosworth, whereupon the priest set about making such changes in it as would be likely to please the new King. The copy which had passed out of his hands probably gave him some anxious moments, but he did what he could to give the remaining *Roll* an orthodox Lancastrian tone. The passage praising Richard is cut out and he is described merely as the 'infelix maritus' of Anne Neville. Anne herself is deprived of some of her royal insignia and a picture of Henry VI is inserted instead of an earlier one of the Duke of Gloucester. Edward IV also disappears. After this editing the mutilated result was ready for Henry Tudor's inspection (*College of Arms*).[31]

Rous is the first, and only strictly contemporary source, to mention any deformity in Richard. Fabyan, the London merchant who must have known him well by sight if not personally, makes no mention of it, neither does the writer of the *Croyland Chronicle* or the Frenchman, de Commines. The good looks of Edward IV and of Clarence are commented on, but none of them draw what would be the obvious comparison if the third brother had been deformed to the point of repulsiveness. His record as a fighter makes it impossible that he should have been a cripple, and there is the traditional testimony of the Countess of Desmond who is reputed to have lived to a great age, and who towards the end of her life recalled that in her youth she had danced with the Duke of Gloucester and that he had been the handsomest man in the room with the exception of his brother Edward. There is also the description of the King by the German, von Poppelau, who visited Richard's court in the spring of 1484 and was given a personal audience. He makes no mention of any physical deformity (*Mancini, tr. Armstrong. Footnote*). Richard appears to have been short like his father the Duke of York and of the slight wiry type who are stronger than they appear to be.

Rous at first merely says that Richard's right shoulder was higher than his left,[32] but this trifling defect was not enough to satisfy Henry, who was well aware that a repulsive physical appearance is easily associated in the public mind with moral degeneracy, and that to the simple a hideous soul is more credible if it is housed in a hideous body. Accordingly Rous, probably at Henry's command, drew a second picture in his *Historia Regum Angliae* which he dedicated to the King. This time he gave full value in a flight of fancy for which there is no sort of corroboration anywhere. Richard's birth itself is described as being abnormal, the child having been two years in his mother's womb from which he eventually emerged with a full set of teeth, hair to his shoulders, talons, a hump back and the right shoulder very much higher than the left.[33]

Here was a monster which might be expected to commit any foul crime and which it would be easy to associate with an atmosphere of nameless evil. In spite of the fact that during Richard's lifetime neither friend nor enemy had ever mentioned this royal monster, who would have been remarkable anywhere, Rous' picture formed the basis for all Tudor historians' descriptions of Richard's personal appearance, though various embellishments, some of them contradictory, were added as they occurred to their authors. The last two pages of Rous' *Historia* are filled with venomous abuse of Richard – to whom he had referred during his lifetime in such glowing terms.

Rous, who died in 1491, wrote within five years of Richard's death, so this description must have been ludicrous to those who had known the King, but, taking the whole of England, these would have been comparatively few in number and would become fewer. It was a good foundation for Henry Tudor to work on. Wanting the definite and spectacular charge which would turn the country against the late King by its horror and having to fall back on a long-term policy of insidious slander, he presented Richard as a creature who could readily be accepted as the perpetrator of atrocious crimes. At best it was a difficult task because throughout his life Richard had been respected as a man of great integrity, loyal, humane, and kindly. In fact, Henry could not have had a more unsatisfactory personality on which to pin a murder of the most despicable kind. He would have to wait, if necessary for years, for it was of the utmost importance to the Tudor dynasty to persuade the world that the two boys were dead.

Patiently Henry and Morton set to work to amplify and propagate the legend which they had conceived.[34] For the lettered, historians were commissioned to rewrite the history of the past few years as Henry wanted it written, and for the ignorant, use was made of popular ballads sung by strolling minstrels, who were then the chief source of entertainment and information for the masses. Richard's supposed misdeeds and the just retribution meted out to him by that instrument of divine justice, Henry Tudor, were sung up and down the country.

Some of these ballads have survived, the best known being 'The Song of the Lady Bessie', the work of one Humphrey Brereton, a squire in the household of Lord Stanley, now the Earl of Derby. This purports to tell the story of Richard's crimes and of the Stanley-Tudor conspiracy which brought about his downfall. It accuses Richard roundly of the murder of his nephews and of his Queen, for which acts he is universally hated. The Lady Bessie is of course Elizabeth of York, who is represented as being the instigator of the plot. She persuades Lord Stanley to write letters to his brother Sir William Stanley, to Sir John Savage, and to Gilbert Talbot, asking assistance in bringing Henry Tudor over the sea to marry her and to become King. The ballad describes the negotiations between the conspirators in detail and ends with the battle of Bosworth, the death of Richard, and the bringing of his body to Leicester, where the Lady Bessie jeers at it in a singularly unpleasant but fortunately apocryphal passage. Finally Bessie is married to Henry by the Archbishop of Canterbury, after which Stanley places the crown on their heads. This epic was designed to please the King and to appeal to the ignorant. Doubtless it fulfilled both aims.

The contemporary chroniclers whose work has survived are all Tudor and Lancastrian in sympathy who set down their narratives during Henry's reign. Such a one was Fabyan, a leading citizen and an alderman of London. That part of his chronicle which deals with the reigns of Edward IV and Richard III is superficial and confused as regards the sequence of events while his dating is hopelessly inaccurate. He hardly treats at all of happenings outside London, where he lived, but he *is* the first to suggest that Edward of Lancaster was murdered after Tewkesbury (' . . . by the King's servants incontinently slain'). He does not connect anyone by name with the deed.[35]

He accuses Richard of direct responsibility for the death of Henry VI, quoting 'common fame' as his authority. This is the first record of a rumour which Fabyan admits is only one of the 'divers tales' told of Henry's end.[36] Of the young princes he writes that they were put 'under sure keeping' in the Tower and that they 'never came abroad', though he was not necessarily in a position to know whether they did or not. Later he again quotes 'common fame' as reporting that their uncle had 'put them to secret death', but he obviously has no real knowledge of their fate. As an example of his inaccuracy, he gives Thursday June 20th as the date of Richard's accession and the 21st as the day of his proclamation. In this he is a week out, as Richard was proclaimed King on Thursday, June 26th. He has not even got the days of the week right, as the 20th and 21st were Friday and Saturday respectively in 1483. He had no excuse for this inaccuracy as he was himself in London at the time; a man who is unreliable in matters of common knowledge cannot be believed on more obscure and important ones. He records popular rumours which, being a Lancastrian, he wanted to believe.

VII

UNEASY CROWN

*I*n 1489 Henry had a further disturbing indication of his own unpopularity and of the affection which the north still retained for Richard. The Earl of Northumberland, who had betrayed his King at Bosworth, was murdered by the Yorkshiremen at Thirsk while attempting to collect taxes for Henry, who was obliged to send a considerable force to put down the disturbance. This reminder that his hold on the sceptre was still precarious coincided with a renewed outbreak of the rumour that at least one of Edward IV's sons was alive.

In 1491 the rumours crystallized into hard fact in the shape of a new and much more dangerous claimant to the throne. Again backed by Margaret of Burgundy, a young man hitherto known as Perkin Warbeck announced that he was in reality Richard Duke of York and the rightful King of England. He bore a remarkable resemblance to his supposed father Edward IV and showed an extraordinarily intimate knowledge of court matters which were not generally known. Either he was in fact the missing boy or he had been extremely well coached in his part. Like his predecessor Lambert Simnel he launched his bid for the throne from Ireland, but unlike Simnel he was not so easily disposed of.

He was recognized at one time or another by the Kings of France, Denmark and Scotland, by the Duke of Saxony and the Emperor Maximilian. The King of Scotland gave him his cousin, the Lady Catherine Gordon, for wife, and later provided him with an army to invade England. His likeness to Edward IV makes it probable that if he were not the Duke of York he was at least an illegitimate son of that promiscuous monarch. In England the news of his claim was received with acclamation and intense excitement. In Bacon's vivid words the news that the real Duke of York was about to claim his inheritance ' . . . came blazing and thundering over into England'.

The supposed murders in the Tower went by the board, showing that they had never been seriously believed and that the people were only too ready to discard a story which had never been proved or indeed attained higher status than ordinary gossip. People of all classes were delighted to accept the tidings that the Duke of York was alive, though Elizabeth Woodville could no longer intrigue on her son's behalf, having recently died in poverty in her enforced retreat at Bermondsey.[37]

Henry took immediate and characteristic steps to discourage his nobles from supporting Warbeck. He employed a certain Sir Robert Clifford to offer his services to Warbeck in Burgundy with orders to worm himself into the innermost councils of the pretender, and as a result of the information thus obtained Henry pounced on several prominent men among his own followers, chief among them being Sir William Stanley, to whom, with his brother, now Earl of Derby, he was principally indebted for his crown. It seems that Henry had been doubtful of Sir William's loyalty for the past three years, possibly because he realized that a man who had betrayed one master could equally well betray another. Now he had the evidence he needed to bring a charge of high treason against his step-uncle, which resulted in Sir William's execution. One of the principal counts against Stanley was that he had been heard to say that if he could be sure that Warbeck was the son of Edward IV nothing would induce him to bear arms against him. Not, be it noticed, whether the son of Edward IV was still alive, but only whether this particular youth were he. Stanley himself seems to have had small belief in the supposed murders.

The Warbeck affair dragged on for seven years, and only Warbeck's own cowardice and incompetence were responsible for his ultimate downfall. Gradually the enthusiasm which had greeted the news of his coming died away for lack of encouragement, but throughout those years Henry was subjected to a ceaseless anxiety whose roots lay in his inability to discover the real fate of Edward's sons. Warbeck fell into his hands at last and was finally lodged in the Tower, where Henry made use of him to dispose of the unfortunate Earl of Warwick, who had spent the fourteen years since Bosworth in close confinement there. Failing the sons of Edward IV, he was the last Plantagenet heir to the throne. Henry was anxious to negotiate a marriage between his eldest son and the Infanta Catherine of Spain, but the Spaniards refused to consider such an alliance while there was any doubt of the Tudor dynasty's title.[38] Henry therefore trumped up a charge against both Warbeck and Warwick which accused them of plotting to escape. Warbeck was hanged at Tyburn and Warwick was beheaded on Tower Hill.

Henry breathed again, but the anxieties of the past years had made him desperate to prevent the appearance of any more pretenders. It was imperative that a plausible account of the fate of the children should be given out to the world. Twice in fifteen years his throne had been shaken by claimants; some explanation and if possible a scapegoat had to be found before a third appeared. Henry at last discovered the man who could be made to supply both, and his name was James Tyrell.

Sir James Tyrell of Gipping had been a trusted servant of both Edward IV and Richard III. He had been knighted after the battle of Tewkesbury, had served on a commission for discharging the office of Lord High Constable and had been Master of the Horse under Edward, which latter office he also held under Richard. He had carried out confidential missions for the latter while he was still Duke of Gloucester, and had been made a Knight Banneret by him during the Scottish campaign. After his accession Richard had conferred many other favours on Tyrell, who was altogether a man of considerable standing between 1471 and 1485. In the latter year he was entrusted with some unspecified mission to Flanders which was concerned with 'the King's weal', and at the time of Bosworth he was still abroad at his post as Governor of Guisnes, near Calais. After Henry's usurpation he was deprived of his estates and official posts in Wales and it was some time before he made his peace with the new King. During this period he seems to have remained at Guisnes until in June 1486 he received a general pardon from Henry. This was followed a month later by a second general pardon into which it would be a mistake to read too much significance. He was re-appointed Governor of Guisnes and given land in France instead of his estates in Wales.[39]

Tyrell remained in France for the next sixteen years and nothing further is heard of him until 1502, three years after the deaths of Warwick and Warbeck, when Henry ordered his arrest on a charge of having been in correspondence with the Earl of Suffolk, son of the sister of Edward IV and Richard III. Tyrell refused to submit and prepared to defend himself at Guisnes. Unfortunately he allowed himself to be lured out of the safety of his castle and on board one of

Henry's ships in Calais harbour for a conference. He was promised a safe conduct backed by the personal assurance of the Bishop of Winchester, Lord Privy Seal. Once on board the royal vessel he was shanghaied, taken to England, lodged in the Tower, tried on a vague charge of 'matters of treason' and executed in May 1502.

No sooner was Tyrell safely dead than the King gave out that he had confessed while in prison to the murder on Richard's instructions nineteen years before of the two sons of Edward IV (*Bacon*). The 'confession', as given out verbally by Henry and quoted by More, Bacon, and others, was substantially as follows.[40] After Richard's coronation he set forth on his progress to the north, leaving his nephews in the royal palace at the Tower. He reached his own city of Gloucester at the beginning of August and from there, according to the 'confession', he suddenly sent a messenger, one John Green, to the Constable of the Tower, his old friend Sir Robert Brackenbury, with a letter instructing him to put the two children to death. Brackenbury refused to carry out the order and Green returned with the news of his refusal to Richard, who had by then reached Warwick. Richard, greatly displeased, complained to one of his pages that he could find nobody to do his bidding, whereupon the page suggested that Sir James Tyrell, who was lying on a 'pallet' in the antechamber, would be only too ready to undertake any villainy which might bring him the royal favour and enable him to score off the King's two ministers, Ratcliffe and Catesby, of whom he was intensely jealous. This somewhat casual recommendation is alleged to have been quite enough for the King, who forthwith called for Tyrell and commanded him to ride post-haste to London and do the work which Brackenbury's scruples would not allow him to discharge.

Tyrell, only too pleased to be of service and armed with another letter authorizing him to take over command of the Tower for one night so that he might settle the business undisturbed, posted to London accompanied by his groom, one John Dighton. Arriving at the Tower he presented his remarkable credentials to Brackenbury, who forthwith handed over the keys of his very responsible post to Tyrell, whereupon the latter proceeded to make his arrangements for disposing of the boys during the following night. They were murdered in their beds by John Dighton assisted by two of their attendants, Miles Forrest, apparently a professional murderer, and an individual with the sinister name of Will Slaughter and the equally inauspicious nickname of Black Will. These three did the deed, while Tyrell himself waited outside – a nice touch of refinement. Having smothered the two children the three murderers summoned Tyrell to view the bodies so that he might be assured that they were dead, after which they buried them at the foot of the stairs 'metely deep in the ground under a great heap of stones' (*More*).

Tyrell, having presumably handed the keys back to Brackenbury, rode off to rejoin Richard and to tell him that his instructions had been carried out in an efficient manner, at which Richard 'gave him great thanks and some say made him a knight' (*More*). He had been one since Tewkesbury, but the added touch of an immediate reward is a convincing one.

Richard's only complaint was that the bodies had not been buried in consecrated ground as became the sons of a King, but this omission was easily repaired by having them taken up and re-buried by a priest, who conveniently died shortly afterwards. It happened that Miles Forrest and Will Slaughter also died within a few years, so that of the people supposed to be immediately concerned in the crime only Sir James Tyrell and John Dighton still remained alive nineteen years afterwards to 'confess' to it. As Bacon puts it 'they both agreed in a tale, as the King gave out to this effect'. Neither was tried for this abominable crime, which besides being regicide was the murder of the two brothers of Henry's Queen. Tyrell was executed on another charge before the 'confession' was made public, while John Dighton, 'who it seems spake best for the King', was not only allowed to go free but was given a pension on condition that he lived at Calais, and became the principal means of spreading the story (*Bacon*).

Dead, Tyrell was the perfect scapegoat. Like Richard himself he could not deny anything that might be said about him and there was no call for anything so embarrassing as a trial for regicide. He was also known to have carried out confidential missions for Richard. The whole story was a fantastic farrago of palpable invention produced without any documentary backing nearly twenty years after the events it pretended to relate. If there had been a shadow of truth in such a story why did it take Henry all those years to discover it? Such proceedings as the handing over of the King's palace and principal fortress by its Constable to another man even for a night could hardly have escaped the notice of his subordinates, neither

Henry VI

Edward IV

Elizabeth Woodville

Fotheringhay Castle, a reconstruction of its appearance in the fifteenth century

Richard III, showing signs of alteration of left shoulder line

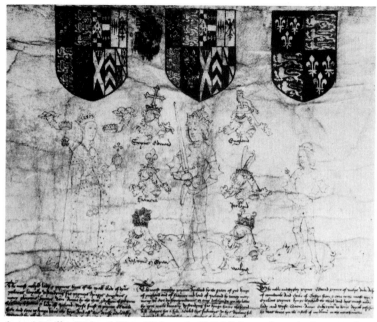

Anne Neville, Richard III and Edward of Middleham, from the Rous Roll, a
contemporary drawing

Middleham Castle

Baynard's Castle, a drawing of the seventeenth century

Crosby Hall, a reconstruction

'Broken Sword' portrait of Richard III, a propaganda picture of the
sixteenth century

'Broken Sword' portrait: X-ray photograph, showing high original
(deformed) shoulder line, and short 'withered' left arm as originally
painted. Later over painting restored the portrait to a more normal
appearance

Henry VII, Pietro Torrigiano bust, from life

could the odd coincidence that from that night the King's nephews had never been seen again. Such a coincidence at a time when rumour was rampant must have given rise to considerable comment which would certainly have reached Henry's ears on his first coming to London after Bosworth, opening the way to a definite condemnation of Richard in the Act of Attainder, and the pursuit and prosecution of the surviving murderers. There was no such comment because there had been nothing to give rise to it; after twenty years Henry, hard driven, felt safe to invent it.

Richard is supposed to have written two letters to Sir Robert Brackenbury, which Sir Robert would have been careful to preserve for his own sake, but no letters were ever produced. Brackenbury himself, who is represented as having rejected with horror his sovereign's command to kill the children, still remained a faithful and trusted servant to the end and died at Bosworth with his master – a circumstance which seems doubly improbable both from his own point of view and from Richard's. A man of conscience would hardly have been likely to follow such a monster to the death, whereas the monster would have taken steps to silence finally a servant who held such a damning secret and who had openly disapproved of the deed. Had Richard intended to murder his nephews for whatever reason, he would hardly have set about it in such a casual manner, writing letters which would have ruined him had they fallen into the wrong hands, to a man of whose obedience in this particular matter he had not made sure beforehand, and apparently without a thought of how he could explain away the disappearance of the children in the years to come. Nobody but an idiot would have set about such a crime in such a way, and it has never been suggested that Richard III was an idiot.

The whole story is a clumsy concoction depending entirely on the fact that all the people mentioned in it were dead by the time it was published (with the exception of Dighton, who was ready to swear to anything in return for immunity and a pension). Brackenbury had died at Bosworth, otherwise it would have been unnecessary to complicate the issue with the tale of his reluctance to commit the crime; he could have been executed on some other charge and posthumously credited with the 'confession' instead of Tyrell. The supposed first and second murderers were dead, so they presented no problem. The priest who was said to have reburied the bodies and died soon afterwards without revealing the grave was obviously invented to account for Henry's failure to find it in the first place, and to prevent officious persons from demanding a search so that the bodies might be re-buried with the ceremony befitting their rank. As it was he had got everything neatly tied up provided his subjects proved sufficiently credulous, and it being as much as their lives and fortunes were worth to be anything else, he had no need to be unduly anxious on that score.

At last Henry had got what he had wanted for so long: some sort of official explanation of the disappearance of the boys whose survival would have made nonsense of his own claim to the throne. He had also something more solid, if only slightly so, than 'common fame' and popular ballads to blacken the name and memory of his rival. From now on Tyrell's 'confession' was made the basis of Richard's story as told by all the Tudor historians, in the same way that Rous' fantastic monster was the basis of all descriptions of his personal appearance. The ground had been painstakingly prepared in the years that had passed since Bosworth and the deliberate dishonouring of Richard's corpse. Patiently, whisper by whisper, and word by word, the legend of the evil mind in the distorted body had been built up until even those still surviving who had known the dead King must have begun to wonder if their own memories were at fault.

It presents an astounding example of what can be achieved by the use of suggestion without one jot of real evidence, and a terrifying instance of the power of inspired propaganda in a totalitarian state. From the date of the 'confession' onwards all references to Richard follow a pattern with which we are only too familiar in our own day [1959]; they read like pronouncements by the Kremlin in full cry after a deviationist.

VIII
THE LEGEND IS ESTABLISHED

*I*n 1502 Henry had occupied the throne of England for seventeen years. He had weathered the storms occasioned by Lambert Simnel, Perkin Warbeck, and his own unpopularity. He had also succeeded in destroying much of the affection which many of his subjects had long continued to entertain for his predecessor. He might have been expected to feel reasonably secure, with sons to follow him and to carry on the Tudor dynasty.

Yet security was something which neither Henry nor any of his immediate descendants ever enjoyed in their hearts. They all suffered in some degree from the inferiority complex of the parvenu who knows that someone else is the rightful possessor of the position which he enjoys, and this sense of insecurity lies behind all the horrifying cruelties of Tudor rule and also explains the unrelenting hatred with which successive Tudors continued to pursue the memory of the last king of the house which they had supplanted, till the monstrous distortion of a man which Henry had invented and fostered became generally accepted.

Henry himself died in 1509. The people forgave him much for the peace which had descended on the country, and indeed they had much to forgive, for Henry's rule had not been a light one. His hand had fallen on all classes, and from the first he ruled as an absolute monarch with a despotism which the country had not known for generations. He was insatiable in the matter of money and his ministers were constantly occupied in devising new ways for squeezing it out of his subjects. Morton, who became Lord Chancellor, Archbishop of Canterbury and a cardinal, invented a new method of assessment for taxation purposes which has gone down in history under the name of 'Morton's Fork'. It had a beautiful simplicity; if a man lived frugally he was presumed to have saved a great deal and to be in a position to give handsomely to the King, whereas if he spent lavishly he was obviously able to do the same. It was, in fact, the most perfect example of 'heads I win tails you lose'.

However, in spite of his avarice, his personal unpopularity and his utter lack of scruple, Henry raised England's prestige, which had begun to climb during Richard's short reign. His subtle mind was a match for his fellow rulers, so that abroad the country commanded more respect than it had done since the days of Henry V. At home the reign was stained with such judicial crimes as the execution of Warwick, and with the establishment of the court of Star Chamber, which has come to be known as the classic example of tyranny, as 'Morton's Fork' has become the synonym of extortion.

Henry succeeded in curbing the power of the nobles by imposing swingeing taxes on the slightest pretext, thus doing the country a real service, for it was no longer menaced by civil commotions caused by the private armies of the nobility. Henry tolerated no power which could rival that of the King, and as he trusted nobody and had his spies everywhere, the most powerful noble lived in dread of drawing that cold and fishy eye upon himself, and of going the way of Sir William Stanley.

To the day of his death Henry's hatred of his predecessor was undiminished. Richard had possessed two things which Henry never had – a sound title to the throne and the love of his subjects. Few people can forgive those they have injured and Henry was not a forgiving man; the older he became, the deeper grew his hatred for the memory of the man on whose throne he sat. He was like an artist who cannot bear to leave his masterpiece but must for ever be adding extra touches to his creation. He had made a legend, but it had to be kept alive, and anything written or spoken to the detriment of Richard was pleasing to the King. At a comparatively early date it must have occurred to someone, probably to Henry himself, that there was something unconvincing in the picture of a man with no previous criminal record but on the contrary an unblemished character, who suddenly committed a revolting pre-meditated crime without an adequate motive; for gradually, first by insinuation and then by downright assertion, responsibility for the death of every prominent person who died during Richard's lifetime was laid on his shoulders till his name emerged as a synonym for evil.

Thus in 1506 Henry commissioned an Italian scholar named Polydore Vergil to write a history of England. Vergil was a native of Urbino who came to England as an assistant collector of the papal tax known as Peter's Pence and attracted the attention of Henry, who presented him to the living of Church Langton and subsequently gave him sundry other ecclesiastical appointments, including that of Archdeacon of Wells. His *Anglica Historia* was begun in 1506 but it was not published till 1534. Henry gave Vergil access to all official records and documents, and it is reported that the historian destroyed wholesale anything which did not agree with the version he wished to present, which was in effect the version acceptable to the Tudors. Whether this is true is uncertain, but bearing in mind Henry's method of dealing with the *Titulus Regius*, it is at least possible.[41]

Vergil is the first writer to implicate Richard of Gloucester in the alleged slaughter of Edward of Lancaster after Tewkesbury. According to him the killing was done in person by the Dukes of Clarence and Gloucester, with Hastings, in the presence of Edward himself. He thus neatly incriminates the three York brothers and their best friend, which from the Tudor point of view would be a great improvement on Fabyan's insinuation which did not name anyone.

Passing on to the supposed murder of Henry VI Vergil writes:

King Edward to the intent that there should be no new insurrections, travelled not long after through Kent, . . . which business being despatched, to the intent every man might conceive a perfect peace to be obtained and that all fear of enemies might be abolished, Henry VI, being not long before deprived of his diadem was put to death in the Tower of London. The continual report is that Richard Duke of Gloucester killed him with a sword whereby his brother might be delivered of all hostility.

Vergil places Henry's death *after* Edward's Kentish expedition whereas the accounts for the unfortunate ex-King's living expenses show that he was certainly dead by May 24th at the latest, before either Edward or Richard returned to London. According to Fabyan it was 'common fame' and according to Vergil 'continual report' which linked Richard's name with the crime. Neither can be regarded as authoritative sources, particularly as Fabyan was writing twenty and Vergil nearly forty years after the event. There is nothing but rumour, and retrospective at that, to connect Richard with Henry's death or with that of his son. Later chroniclers, writing to please their Tudor patrons, linked his name with these two deaths for the obvious reason that his guilt in dastardly crimes at the age of eighteen would make the subsequent villainies with which they wished to load his memory more credible.

Vergil records little that could reflect credit on Richard. There is no mention of his long and faithful service as Governor of the North or of his unshakeable loyalty to Edward. The brilliant Scottish campaign, the success of which was entirely due to Richard's leadership, is dimissed in a few lines and the only credit mention goes to Stanley, who had sat outside Berwick till it surrendered. It is to Vergil, however, that we owe the information that Edward left to Richard the sole charge of the country and his children. This is of the greatest importance, as the fact that he alone had been left responsible at a very difficult crisis is Richard's chief justification for acting as he did when confronted with the Woodville plots. As Vergil is so reluctant to record anything in Richard's favour we may believe that this information is correct and that Edward on his deathbed did leave his younger brother the trust which proved impossible to carry out.

After his experiments in homicide in 1471 Vergil's Richard seems to have lost interest in murder, for it is not until after the death of Edward that any nefarious crime is attributed to him. However, from then onwards he is made to plunge into a veritable blood-bath. Having secretly decided, on receiving the news of his brother's death, to seize the throne at any price, Hastings, Grey, Rivers, Vaughan, Haute,[42] his nephews, innumerable unspecified persons, and finally his own Queen fall victims to his insatiable ambition.

Vergil skates lightly over facts which he twists to suit his own purpose, and over dates and the sequence of events, about which he is totally unreliable, but he seems to have had a remarkably intimate knowledge of Richard's most secret intentions and motives. Thus he asserts that on receiving the news of his brother's death the Duke of Gloucester 'began to be kindled with an ardent desire of sovereignty'. Vergil does not tell us how he obtained this insight into the thoughts of a man dead many years earlier – thoughts which he would have been unlikely to confide to his most trusted friends at the time.

On the contrary, he speaks of Richard's deep dissimulation and of his efforts to hide his intentions. Not seeing his way clear to his desire he 'dissembles' by writing affectionate letters of condolence and reassurance to the Queen, by swearing obedience to his nephew and generally doing all he can to mislead those about him, hoping the while that events would develop in his favour. Then, having gathered 'no small force of armed men' (a mourning train of six hundred gentlemen of the north), he sets off to intercept his nephew, meeting Buckingham on the way, when 'as is commonly believed' he confided to that gentleman his plans for usurping the throne. Together the two dukes catch up with the young King, 'who journeyed on with a small train' (two thousand armed men and his baggage wagons full of weapons), at Stony Stratford, where they forthwith arrest the four nobles, for no reason except that they would oppose Richard's nefarious schemes, and bundle them off to prison at Pontefract.

Notice how very selective Vergil is. He carefully avoids all mention of the Woodville activities in seizing the Tower with its treasure and the Mint, fitting out a naval force and issuing commissions in their own names with no reference to Gloucester, though Vergil himself has told us that Gloucester had been left in sole authority by his brother. His account of the vital seven weeks which followed the arrival of the young King in London is extremely hazy, but his knowledge of the inner workings of the Duke of Gloucester's mind continues to be detailed and remarkable. His narrative of actual events is muddled and vague to a degree which only becomes comprehensible when it is considered how awkward those events were from the point of view of the picture which he wished to paint. He was obliged to pick out those facts or partial facts which suited his story and to furnish motives of which he could have had no knowledge in order to present a result which would be agreeable to his patrons.

Thus there is no mention of the extensive preparations for young Edward's coronation or of the early date, June 22nd, for which this was fixed. He also ignores the fact that the boy signed documents as King up to June 17th.[43] He asserts that Hastings was disposed of as the result of a prepared plot because he disapproved of the Lord Protector's schemes, and not because he had involved himself in plots against Gloucester's authority, though the available evidence shows that this was almost certainly the reason for Hasting's tragic end. The little Duke of York is lodged in the Tower *before* the death of Hastings and not afterwards, as was the case, and he makes the executions of Rivers, Grey, Haute[44] and Vaughan appear as part of the same sinister plot, whereas their trials had been ordered before the Hastings episode, took place under the presidency of the Earl of Northumberland, and resulted in their condemnation and execution on or about June 25th.

As a final distortion he reports Doctor Shaw's sermon as attacking the legitimacy of Edward IV and not that of his sons. It is obvious that this is a quite deliberate lie because Vergil adds '. . . but there is common report that King Edward's children were in that sermon called bastards and not King Edward, which is void of all truth'. That it was not 'void of all truth' but was indeed the reason for the repudiation of the boys by the Lords and Commons is proved both by the *Titulus Regius*, which Vergil believed to have been destroyed, and by the contemporary *Chronicle of Croyland*, of whose existence he was ignorant.[45]

Vergil passes briefly over the other events leading up to Richard's accession and coronation. He omits all mention of the petition which was presented by the Three Estates begging the Duke of Gloucester to accept the crown because of the doubts cast on the legitimacy of Edward's children and to avoid the dangers of a minority. Vergil implies that there was general opposition to Richard's accession, and his magnificent coronation is dismissed in a line: '. . . having assembled together a company of the nobility he was created King at Westminster'. It sounds like a scratch affair attended by the sweepings of the peerage instead of what it was, the most representative gathering at any coronation in the history of England till that date. 'Thus Richard without consent of the commonalty by might and will of certain noblemen of his faction, enjoyed the realm contrary to the law of God and man.'[46]

Vergil and his patrons were very sure the *Titulus Regius* was lost for ever, and they knew that the memories of men are short.

The murder of the two princes is given as an accepted fact, following closely the 'confession' of Sir James Tyrell with the odd reservation that Vergil says that the actual manner of their deaths is unknown. This gives an additional air of mystery to the affair for Tyrell's 'confession' had been very explicit where the supposed murder was concerned. Vergil does not so far commit himself, saying that it was not known by what means the children died. We are back at hearsay sources of 'common fame', and Vergil clings only to the main issue that the children had been killed. He also asserts that the news of their death was given out by Richard himself, which is palpably absurd. The King could never have admitted to their murder, and had the crime taken place their deaths must have been attributed to natural causes, given out officially, and have been followed by the customary exposure of the bodies in St Paul's. Any other method would have been both pointless and politically suicidal.

Vergil gives a heart-rending account of the despair with which Elizabeth Woodville received the news of the death of her sons:

> . . . the news was to the unfortunate mother as it were the very stroke of death . . . forthwith she fell into a swoon and lay lifeless a good while; after coming to herself she weepeth, she cryeth out loud, and with lamentable shrieks maketh the house ring; she struck her breast, tore and cut her hair, and overcome in fine with dolour prayed also her own death . . .

This tragic picture would be even more affecting were it not that six months later the heart-broken mother had made up her quarrel with Richard, given her five daughters into his hands, and from then on remained on the best of terms with the supposed murderer of her sons, being even suspected of going so far as to try to marry her eldest daughter to him when he became a widower a year later! Elizabeth Woodville was throughout her life an accommodating woman when it suited her, but it is beyond belief that she should be as accommodating as this. She was accustomed to turning a blind eye to her husband's peccadilloes but such a habit can surely not become so ingrained that it will extend to overlooking the murder of one's children.

Vergil pays scant attention to Richard's parliament, confining himself to the Acts of Attainder passed on Buckingham and his fellow rebels, and avoiding all mention of that forbidden topic the *Titulus Regius*. The death of Richard's son is given as having taken place three months after his installation as Prince of Wales at York in 1483 instead of after the ratification of his title by parliament in 1484, and the rebellion of Buckingham is placed after the boy's death instead of nine months before. It will be seen that Vergil, whether by design or through ignorance, is thoroughly unreliable even where well authenticated events are concerned. He is far more interested in the plots to bring Henry Tudor to England and gives much more space to the peregrinations of that young man in France and Brittany than he does to events in England.

Henry is always represented as the gallant young hero destined by divine Providence to save England from the grip of the bloody tyrant Richard, whose every action is attributed to the basest motives. His good government is an attempt to win back the popularity he has lost by murdering his nephews, if he is generous he is trying to curry favour, his magnanimity towards his enemies is hypocrisy, his kindly actions are nothing but deep dissimulations to cover his evil deeds. The whole narrative appears to have been written with the intention of obscuring the truth, but Vergil defeats his own aim. The picture he draws approaches the ludicrous, ignoring possibility, let alone probability. The mud is laid on so thick that the figure of the man ceases to bear any resemblance to a credible human being. The description of Richard's person is typical:

> He was little of stature, deformed of body, the one shoulder being higher than the other, a short and sour countenance which seemed to savour of mischief and deceit. The while he was thinking of any matter he did continually bite his nether lip as though that cruel nature of his did so rage against itself in that little carcase.

When Vergil's history was printed in 1534 Richard had been dead for fifty years. There can have been few people still living who could remember him personally and the picture of an evil hunchbacked deformity who had waded through blood to a usurped throne was generally accepted. It would have been ill-advised to question it with Henry Tudor's son on the throne, who had no more love for the remaining Plantagenets than his father had had, and not a whisper of contradiction has come down to us. Among the chroniclers each writer copied from his predecessor, adding what embellishments occurred to him to the main outline. It was safer that way.[47]

IX

SIR THOMAS MORE

*R*ous, Fabyan, and Vergil with Henry himself as their inspiration had done their work well, but the worst blow to Richard's reputation came after Henry's death through the medium of a man whose personal integrity has given weight to everything with which his name is connected. This man was Thomas More, who, as a youth, had entered the household of John Morton, the Lord Chancellor, Archbishop of Canterbury, a cardinal, and Henry's principal adviser.

Years later, after Sir Thomas More, as he then was, had been executed by Henry VIII for refusing to countenance his master's matrimonial intentions with regard to Anne Boleyn and his subsequent claim to be head of the Church of England, an unfinished fragment was found among his papers and published by More's son-in-law, Rastell, with the following foreword:

> The History of Richard III (unfinished) written by Master Thomas More, then one of the under-Sheriffs of London about the year 1513 Which work hath been before this time printed in Hardyng's Chronicle and in Hall's Chronicle, but very much corrupt in many places sometime having less and sometime having more and altered in words and whole sentences, much varying from the copy in his own hand, by which this is printed.

It will thus be seen that the genesis and history of this work is very obscure, but there are certain pointers which give us a good indication of its origin. In the first place More himself was born about 1480. He was therefore a child at the time of Bosworth, and not in a position to have any first-hand knowledge of the events which he relates. He must have got his information, true or false, from someone else, and it is a fair assumption, which is supported from internal evidence, that that someone was Morton.

It has even been suggested that Morton was the author of the fragment, and that Thomas More had begun to make a copy of the manuscript which he had laid aside half finished. It is continued in Hardyng's *Chronicle*, which carries the story on to the death of Richard.[48] Thus it is possible that the whole originally existed in a manuscript by Morton, though it must have been added to by others as it refers to events after his death. Buck, writing in the seventeenth century, inclines to the theory of Morton's authorship for he says that 'Doctor Morton made the book and Master More . . . set it forth, amplifying it and glossing it.' This is borne out by the description of certain events at which Morton is known to have been present. One of these is the death of Edward IV, which is graphically described. The author relates how Edward, propped up with pillows, made his appeal to his nobles and then '. . . no longer enduring to sit up laid him down on his left side, his face toward them'. Nobody could doubt that this is the account of someone who had been present.

Whether Morton was the author or the inspiration of the work known as More's *History of Richard III*, he was certainly its source, and a more tainted source for any evidence concerning Richard it would be impossible to find. It can lay no claim to credence because of More's own reputation for integrity, though that is not to say that when he wrote or copied it he did not himself sincerely believe in the truth of what he had been told by a patron who was probably held in veneration by the youth in his teens. It is no reflection on More, a young man of twenty when Morton died, that he should have accepted that prelate's account of events which happened when he himself was a small child, but later historians are gravely to blame in allowing the reputation for integrity and virtue which More subsequently acquired to blind them to the circumstances under which this early and incomplete fragment was written. At the distance of centuries it is easier to assess the value or otherwise of a version owing its origin to the foremost Tudor propagandist.

The main outlines of the story as told by More and the anonymous continuator of Hardyng's *Chronicle*, are substantially the same as Polydore Vergil's version.[49] They were all written at about the same time though they were not printed till much later. Each varies in certain particulars as is to be expected in a narrative derived from 'common fame', but the version attributed to More is much better written and more detailed. It abounds with those irrelevant but circumstantial details which make it far more convincing than Vergil's dry history and which, besides indicating that the original narrator was frequently an eye-witness, shows that he was also possessed of a fertile imagination and a mind that was fully aware of the convincing value of detail on occasions when he could not possibly have been present.

According to More or Morton, Richard had already been plotting to seize the crown during Edward's lifetime. The idea seems to have occurred to him at a very early age when there was not only Edward and the whole of his large family between him and the throne but Clarence and his two children as well. This would certainly have shown considerable enterprise in Richard and a quite remarkable faculty for long-term planning. To make this statement a little more plausible the writer suggests, and this is absolutely the first time that such a thing was even hinted at, that Richard was in some way responsible for the death of Clarence. The passage in which this insinuation is made is a model of how to state a fact and at the same time to imply the opposite:

Some wise men also ween that his drift covertly conveyed lacked not in helping forth his brother Clarence to his death; which he resisted openly howbeit somewhat (as men deemed) more faintly than he that were heartily minded to his weal. And they that thus deem think that he long time in King Edward's life forethought to be King in case that the King his brother (whose life he looked that evil diet should shorten) should happen to decease (as indeed he did) while his children were still young; and they deem that for this intent he was glad of his brother's death the Duke of Clarence, whose life must needs have hindered him so intending whether the same Duke of Clarence had kept him true to his nephew the young King or enterprised to be King himself. But of all this point there is no certainty, and who divineth upon conjectures may as well shoot too far as too short.

The only definite statement in this whole paragraph is that Richard 'resisted openly' – in other words that he protested against Clarence's execution, but by the time the writer has finished with his 'wise men' and their 'deeming' and 'weening' the reader has the impression of a dark plot on Richard's part to get Clarence out of the way on the chance that at some later date Edward might eat, drink, and womanize himself into his grave before his children were grown up. This sounds so like Morton's devious mind that it almost fixes the authorship of at least the early part of the fragment.

On receiving the news of Edward's death Richard is credited with a fortnight of really remarkable activity. He contrives a plot to prevent the young King from coming to London with a large escort, although away in the north he could not even have heard of such an intention let alone have taken steps to prevent it. He writes letters to the Queen, to Buckingham, to Hastings, to all sorts of people, receives answers, acts on them, and writes more letters. The to-ing and fro-ing attributed to him in a couple of weeks would have taxed modern resources and in the fifteenth century it would have been quite impossible.

Typical of the kind of 'evidence' cited by Sir Thomas More is the following incident:

> . . . this I have by credible information learned, that the self-same night in which King Edward died, one Mistlebrook long ere morning came in great haste to the house of one Potter dwelling in Red Cross Street without Cripplegate, and when he was with hasty rapping quickly letten in he showed unto Potter that King Edward was departed. 'By my troth' quoth Potter 'then will my master the Duke of Gloucester be king.'

However 'credible' Sir Thomas may have thought it, this anecdote means exactly nothing. We do not know who Potter was or how much his surmises are likely to have been worth.[50] He was probably a court hanger-on who knew something of the intrigues surrounding the late King and of the ambition and unpopularity of the Woodvilles, and with a dash of wishful thinking and a certain shrewd prescience he forecast what actually happened and saw his master King of England. More, who evidently knew little of Potter himself, adds:

> What cause he had so to think hard it is to say, whether he being toward him anything knew that he such a thing purposed, or otherwise had any inkling thereof, for he was not likely to speak it of nought.

Here the good Sir Thomas shows himself singularly naïve, for in fact Potter was very likely to have said something of the kind 'of nought'. It is the typical remark of the self-important man who likes to appear possessed of inside information, whereas it is not at all the sort of thing that a trusted confidential servant who might have some such knowledge would blurt out to someone who came hammering on the door in the middle of the night. Such backstairs gossip and garbage-tin raking do More little credit.

Subsequent pages are devoted to long arguments between the Queen and the lords sent to induce her to part with the Duke of York, the Lord Protector with his sinister intentions being the moving spirit who made use of the innocent nobles and the Archbishop of Canterbury to get the boy into his clutches. On the whole the main events up to this point are not in dispute. It is the construction put on them and the motives attributed to Richard which are unconfirmed by any evidence and against all probability.

This is particularly evident in the vivid account of the scene in the council chamber at the Tower which ended in the summary execution of Hastings. The writer has already told us that the Lord Protector was doubtful of Hastings' loyalty to himself and had deputed Catesby, a lawyer who had received many favours from the Lord Chamberlain, to sound him. Catesby appears to have been engaged in some devious double-dealing, for Hastings was at the same time employing him to spy on the Lord Protector. In the small hours of the morning of June 13th Lord Stanley sent an urgent message to Hastings saying that he had had a nightmare in which he saw a wild boar (Richard's cognisance) savaging them both. He said he had horses ready and urged Hastings to fly with him immediately. Hastings, having somewhat stronger nerves, replied that flight would be to court danger and advised Stanley to pay no heed to dreams. It seems clear from this episode that Hastings and Stanley were engaged in some plot against the Lord Protector, and had guilty consciences. Later someone, almost certainly Catesby, who is described as 'a meane man at that time but now of great authority', came to fetch Hastings to the meeting at the Tower. Here we have another indication of Morton's connection with the work, for Catesby rose to be one of Richard's most trusted ministers, but was beheaded by Henry after Bosworth. This part of the history must therefore have been written up from notes made by Morton during his exile and Richard's lifetime.

The description of the actual meeting in the council chamber bears every mark of the eye-witness with a subtle skill in mixing truth with falsehood and a definite aim to convey a desired impression. More fulfils neither of these conditions, but Morton does in both respects.

He describes how Richard entered the chamber at nine o'clock in the morning in genial spirits, asking for a 'messe' of the excellent strawberries which he had seen in the Bishop of Ely's garden in Holborn. After a short time he leaves the room. He returns about an hour later with a very changed appearance, 'with a wonderful sour countenance, knitting his brows, frowning and fretting and gnawing his lips', and after an uneasy pause bursts out with an accusation against the Queen and Jane Shore, the late King's mistress, who was now under the protection of Hastings. Pulling up his sleeve he declares that they had withered his arm and demands what punishment should be meted out to them. Hastings replies that if that is the case they are worthy of heinous punishment, whereupon Richard rounds upon him, accusing him also of treason and smiting the table with his fist, at which the guard rushes in and at his orders arrests Hastings, Stanley, Morton, and Rotherham, Archbishop of York. The three latter are removed to prison, but Richard orders Hastings to immediate execution, swearing that he will not dine till his erstwhile friend's head is off.

He then sends for the Lord Mayor and with Buckingham receives him in hastily donned armour, telling him of a plot only revealed that morning to murder himself and his cousin at the council table, Hastings being the ringleader of the conspiracy.

This is such a famous scene, of which the only account is that contained in More's *Life of Richard III*, that it is worth while examining it in some detail. Whatever the source of the rest of More's *Life of Richard III*, it is quite certain that the description and interpretation of this scene comes from Morton, who was one of the principal actors in it. The general outline is undoubtedly correct; Richard did arrive in good spirits, he did return after his temporary absence in a towering passion, he did accuse the Woodvilles, Stanley, Hastings, Morton and Rotherham of plotting against his authority and his life, and he did order Hastings' summary execution. Morton puts his own construction on these events: Richard had planned a *coup d'état* and his pleasant manner was assumed to put his victims off their guard. He had Hastings murdered because Hastings was opposed to his nefarious schemes and his receiving of the Lord Mayor in rusty armour was an act designed to justify his proceedings to the citizens of London on the grounds of extreme urgency.

This is the story which Morton and his master Henry Tudor wanted believed. It was part and parcel of all their propaganda both before and after Richard's death, and of a piece with the eventual story of the murders in the Tower. It is however capable of quite another and far more probable interpretation. Richard was faced with a new and explosive situation created by the revelation of the illegitimacy of Edward's children which had been made known to the council by Stillington. He had to find out whom he could trust and he set Catesby to sound his old friend Hastings as to the extent he could rely on him in whatever course he decided to take.

Stanley's acute attack of nerves the night before the Tower meeting is fully explained if indeed he and Hastings were plotting the murder of the Lord Protector the next morning. In the meantime Catesby, who was also trusted by Hastings, has discovered the scope of the plot which was so imminent. He goes to fetch Hastings himself, perhaps to learn the final details. Richard in the meantime, anxious but ignorant of his friend's perfidy, arrives at the meeting in good humour. He is called out of the room by Catesby and is away more than an hour, when he returns having learnt the worst. More's (or Morton's) description is that of a man who has received a sudden and terrible shock and is fighting to retain his self-control. It is not that of someone who is bringing a deep-laid plot to its successful culmination. The reference to the withered arm must on every outside piece of evidence be an invention which probably has its origin in some words of Richard's to the effect that the Woodville plots had paralysed his arm – quite a likely metaphor. It was probably inserted in the physical sense to agree with Rous' description of a deformed cripple.[51]

Richard's treatment of the conspirators is in keeping with the sudden discovery of a plot and the feeling of horror inspired in him at his betrayal by his friend. Hastings is the only one to lose his life, and that with a disregard of the forms of justice very uncharacteristic of Richard. Stanley was released within three weeks, Rotherham within a few months, and Morton was given into the charge of the Duke of Buckingham and played a prominent part in the later subversion of that nobleman. It is as though the disgust and revulsion which Richard felt at this betrayal by his personal friend was such that it could only be assuaged by Hastings' immediate death. Richard behaved in much the same way six months later when he refused to grant the equally false Buckingham a last interview before he was executed.

When Richard told the Lord Mayor that he had only learnt the details of the plot that same morning he was probably speaking the exact truth. The fact that Morton assumes it to be a lie is no reason to believe that such was the case. It is merely the version which suits Morton.

As in Vergil's account the executions of Rivers and his companions are made to take place on the same day as that of Hastings, thereby implying that they are all part of the same preconceived plot. In fact these executions did not take place for another ten days, Rivers' will being dated the 23rd June.

There is one other significant point at which More's history differs from any other of the period. This is in the description of Shaw's sermon, where he departs from the story as told by Vergil, or indeed by anyone else, drawing an entirely new red herring across the trail. He names Elizabeth Lucy as the lady with whom Edward IV was alleged to have gone through a ceremony of marriage prior to that with Elizabeth Woodville. That this is untrue we know from the subsequently discovered draft[52] of the *Titulus Regius* and from the *Croyland Chronicle*, both of which name the Lady Eleanor Butler, and the fact that anyone should have gone to the trouble of recording a deliberate lie is highly significant, particularly as the account is most circumstantial. The writer tells how the Duchess of York, mother of Edward, in an endeavour to stop the Woodville marriage, tried to force Elizabeth Lucy to swear that there had been a pre-contract between herself and the King, and how the lady had refused to take a sacred oath and had finally confessed that although the King had seduced her under promise of marriage there had in fact been no legal contract between them, and in consequence there had been no impediment to the Woodville marriage.

Now, nobody had at any time suggested that Edward was ever contracted to Elizabeth Lucy. She had been his mistress openly for many years and had had two children by him whom he had recognized. What conceivable reason could there be for setting up this cock-shy in order to knock it down again except the sufficiently good one that this story could be demonstrated to be false, whereas the *true* pre-contract with Eleanor Butler was a fact which could be – and had been – proved, thus making the Woodville marriage invalid, the children of it illegitimate, and the claim of Richard of Gloucester to the throne a rightful one, as parliament had declared? The Tudor propagandists had over-reached themselves, and unknowingly provided the strongest proof of that which they were so anxious to disprove. They were so sure that the *Titulus Regius* was lost for ever and its contents 'out of memory and forgot' that they felt safe to embroider.[53] By protesting too much his enemies confirmed Richard's title more surely than ever his friends were able to do.

From this point the narrative agrees closely with Vergil's. The story of the murder of the two boys is similar, though told with more detail and certainly by More himself, and is based on Tyrrel's 'confession' as given out verbally by Henry. More tells the tale 'not after every way that I have heard, but after that way that I have so heard and by such means as methinketh it were hard but it should be true' and being a just man he feels bound to add 'whose death and final infortune hath natheless so far come in question that *some yet remain in doubt whether they were in his (Richard's) days destroyed or no'* (my italics). Which leaves the whole question in the air.

Evidently in spite of the many rumours he had heard More was not certain in his own mind that Richard was guilty. All his information was based on hearsay, and though much of it came from his old patron – 'them that much know and had little cause to lie' – as a lawyer himself he would know the danger of hearsay evidence, even though he might not realize how much cause the ex-Bishop of Ely had to lie.

The fragment in More's handwriting breaks off abruptly in the middle of Morton's talks with Buckingham at Brecknock, in which Morton appears, perhaps not surprisingly, in a rather better light than in other accounts of these negotiations. The history, continued by Hardyng[54] who carries it up to the death of Richard, ends with a description of his appearance and character which is almost word for word the same as Vergil's. There is much evidence to show that these historians drew their material from a common source which may have been a manuscript of Morton's, and that they borrowed from each other what they did not invent for themselves.

X

THE LATER TUDORS

*W*hen Henry VII died in 1509 he had successfully disposed of all the known living members of the House of York with the exception of the Earl of Suffolk and the Countess of Salisbury, daughter of Clarence.[55] Shortly before his death he managed to get Suffolk into his hands, pledging his royal word for his safety. Either Henry had not the courage to break this oath himself or he died before he could frame a charge by which he could justify a judicial murder, but on his deathbed he left an order to his son that he should put Suffolk to death. Henry VIII, nothing loath, carried out his father's instructions and another member of the unlucky family met his end on the scaffold.

In 1541, as the result of a further outbreak of Plantagenet phobia, the seventy-year-old Countess of Salisbury was executed on a trumped-up charge of treason, being literally hacked to death on the scaffold in one of the most hideous scenes recorded in history. That her son, Reginald Pole, did not share her fate was only due to his prudence in keeping out of harm's way in Italy, where he became a cardinal. For all practical purposes the Tudors had now succeeded in their aim to exterminate the family whose throne they had usurped. Compared to their record Richard's supposed crimes pale into insignificance. Yet Richard has gone down to history as a monster, while the Tudors, father and son, are looked on, the one as dull and miserly but respectable, and the other as Bluff King Hal, uncomfortable as a husband certainly, but otherwise not a bad sort.

The picture of Richard III which the first Tudor had inspired and fostered had now, as he intended, passed into recorded history and been accepted. Fifty years had gone by since a mangled corpse had been exposed naked to the jeering mob outside the Greyfriars at Leicester and even the beggarly tomb which Henry had belatedly put up over the bones of the last Plantagenet king had vanished, demolished with the Greyfriars church itself by Henry VIII's church-breakers. The very few still living who had known Richard as he really was dared not court trouble by questioning the official version, and amid so much bloodshed the slander of a long-dead man could have been of little account to the living. It was perpetuated by each successive chronicler, Hall and Holinshed, both of whom took their material from More, Vergil and Hardyng, adding extra details of their own invention; Holinshed added the name of Dorset to the supposed murderers of Edward of Lancaster.

The years went by and the legend became more firmly established, until at the end of the sixteenth century a man who was not an historian at all put the final seal on it, ensuring that it should be perpetuated in our literature as well as our history. In 1593 or thereabouts William Shakespeare wrote a play about Richard, and he lifted the material for his play bodily from Holinshed's chronicle.

It has been said that the English take their religion from Milton and their history from Shakespeare, and certainly for every person who has troubled to search the original records for the real Richard there are many thousands who have seen the murderous hunchback on the stage and have accepted what they have seen for indisputable fact. This extraordinary credulity is not confined to those who are not interested in historical truth and who never read source history for themselves. Scholars and historians of standing will quote Shakespeare with childlike faith, not as a poet and playwright but as a fellow historian. Dr Gairdner, in the preface of his *Lancaster and York*, writes:

For the period of English history treated in this volume we are fortunate in possessing an unrivalled interpreter in our great dramatic poet Shakespeare. A regular sequence of historical plays exhibits to us not only the general character of each successive reign but nearly the whole chain of leading events from the days of Richard II to the death of Richard III at Bosworth. Following the guidance of such a master mind we realise for ourselves the men and actions of the period in a way we cannot do in any other epoch.

This astounding claim for Shakespeare's pretensions as an historian would undoubtedly have caused Shakespeare himself considerable surprise and amusement. In his own day he was not considered to be an authority on anything. He was not even The Bard or Our Great Dramatic Poet. He was simply a working playwright with a living to make, and his first consideration was what was likely to be pleasing to his patrons and the public. The Elizabethans liked their villains to be villainous and there was a constant demand for a really bloody gangster play just as today there is a similar demand for a sadistic gangster film. Shakespeare's Richard was nothing but a royal gangster who had been presented to him ready-made by the Tudor chroniclers.

Shakespeare was in no way concerned with historical accuracy in this or any of the 'histories'. He made his facts fit his plays and he shifted events backwards and forwards in time to suit his convenience and the exigencies of the theatre. It was of no consequence to him that he presented Richard as a grown man revelling in bloodshed at the battle of Towton (*Henry VI, Part 3*), when at that time he was in fact a child of eight living in exile at Utrecht, or that he made Clifford murder a child Earl of Rutland when in fact Rutland was a young man of seventeen who died fighting at the battle of Wakefield. Or that he made Margaret of Anjou, Henry VI's widow, wander about the palace of Westminster prophesying woe on Richard in 1483 when in fact she had been ransomed and sent back to France in 1475. Or that he invented a Machiavellian plot on the part of Richard to bring about the death of Clarence for which there was no previous evidence at all. None of these were historical facts; they were merely good theatre and as such the playwright made use of them.

Shakespeare was not a research worker who delved into records in order to ensure that his characters were historically correct, or even credible. That was not his business, and there was no reason why he should spoil a very satisfactory villain which had been presented to him by the chroniclers. The granddaughter of Henry VII was on the throne, and who was Shakespeare, dependent on court favour for his livelihood, to attack the portrait of the last Plantagenet king which Henry himself had painted? Such an action is not in the least likely to have even occurred to Shakespeare, who took Richard as he found him in Tudor chronicles, telescoped the years to fit the action of the play so that he could get in all the gory murders of which Richard had ever been accused, including that of Clarence of which he had not, clothed the whole in immortal verse, and presented the stage with one of its plum parts and the world with an unforgettable picture of evil incarnate under the name of Richard III. That he was perpetuating a most devastating distortion of a human being probably never occurred to him and it is unlikely that he would have been particularly troubled if it had.

But that play has become the most formidable indictment of Richard, a propagandist's dream of which even Henry Tudor had never thought. Even if it were possible after so many years to clear his name beyond all shadow of doubt, it would still, because of Shakespeare's smash-hit, remain a synonym for evil to the majority. Now that cinema and television have brought Shakespeare to a wider audience the legend has spread still further. That is the way popular history is made, today as in the fifteenth and sixteenth centuries.

Crown in Thorn Bush

XI

AFTER THE TUDORS

*I*n 1603, one hundred and eighteen years after Richard's death, Elizabeth, last of the Tudors, died.

A few years later the original draft of the *Titulus Regius* was discovered among some forgotten documents in the Tower.[56] Speed printed it in his *History* in 1611. Whether it was the light which this discovery threw on the true facts concerning Richard's accession and on Henry's duplicity, or whether it was now safe to deviate from the Tudor line, the hitherto accepted version of Richard's story began to be questioned. Sir William Cornwallis wrote a treatise, *In Praise of King Richard*,[57] and in 1646 Sir George Buck published a spirited defence of the King, in his *History of King Richard III*.

Buck came of a Yorkist family and one of his ancestors, Sir John Buck, had been an official of Richard's household and had fought for him at Bosworth, so that it is possible that the version of events which his descendant wrote was based on tradition which had been handed down in the family.[58] In an official position at Richard's court John Buck would have been able to gain much inside information about his master's affairs. If this information had been preserved it would be far more likely to be near the truth than the subsequent accounts of men who had not even been in the country at the time and who wrote on royal instructions many years later. Buck's history is Yorkist in tone as opposed to the Lancastrian-Tudor bias of other histories, but its claim to authenticity is not lessened by that. He at least had no personal axe to grind in striving to clear the name of his ancestor's master and King.

Sir George Buck's history is in five books and throughout he writes in terms of the highest praise of Richard's good qualities both as man and as King. 'His wisdom and courage had not then their nickname and calumny as now, but drew the eyes and the acknowledgement of the whole kingdom towards him.'

The revolutionary writings of Cornwallis and Buck began the controversy as to the truth about the life and character of Richard III which has continued ever since. Subsequent historians such as Rapin and Carte find themselves unable to accept the Tudor story in its entirety. Carte in particular is very fair, and, while he does not feel able to clear Richard completely, he gives him full credit for his virtues both before and after his accession as well as for his good government and for the excellent and equitable laws passed by his only parliament. He treats the story of the murder of the princes with contempt as ' . . . a mere point of conjecture . . . this story was first invented and given out by the Lancastrians when it was necessary for their purpose at the time of the Duke of Buckingham's insurrection.' This view is certainly supported by all the ascertainable facts.

Rapin, writing in the early eighteenth century, admits that the Tudor chroniclers had done Richard less than justice and adds that ' . . . one cannot help observing in their writings a very strong desire to please the monarchs then on the throne', which seems to be putting it very mildly. On the other hand, he cannot bring himself to discard such improbable stories as the slander of the Duchess of York in Dr Shaw's sermon and the murder of Richard's own wife, and he gives as an unqualified fact the Tudor version of the death of the two princes in the Tower.

However, doubts had begun to creep in and the next writer to enter the lists on Richard's behalf was the redoubtable Horace Walpole, whose brilliant and witty *Historic Doubts on the Reign of Richard III* caused a considerable disturbance in historical circles and involved the writer in an acrimonious dispute with sundry learned men of his day, including Hume, who came out strongly on the Tudor side. Hume accepted the Tudor stories without question, as did Lingard, with a credulity and a lack of any critical faculty deplorable in so distinguished an historian, but in the nineteenth century there was a further strong revulsion against the crudity of the traditional version. Bayley, Laing, Courtenay, Halsted, Legge, Sharon Turner and Jesse all reject the allegations against Richard in whole or in part.

Dr Gairdner devoted many years and great erudition to consideration of the period and of the problem of Richard in particular.

The result, in his *Life and Reign of Richard III*, is a remarkable and puzzling production.

In his preface he admits that he had been troubled for many years by doubts as to Richard's guilt but that he had been unable to discard as baseless something which was so deeply rooted in tradition. In his main work he draws the portrait of a man of honour, integrity, and wisdom, against whom there was no breath of scandal for the first thirty years of his life, but who, for no reason which could be called even remotely adequate, suddenly commits a crime of the most revolting, sordid, and idiotic nature.

Dr Gairdner says, 'The malign tradition itself is not well accounted for, and we are not entirely shown that the story of Richard's life is more intelligible without it.' This seems an astounding statement from the standpoint of plain common sense, for the malign tradition *is* completely accounted for by Henry Tudor's characteristic motive, expediency, and the urgent necessity which compelled him and his successors to use every means in their power in order to destroy the popularity of the House of York, and also to produce some explanation which would dispose of the sons of Edward IV and their claim to the throne, which Henry himself had restored. It is impossible to imagine two stronger motives for Henry, being the man he was and in the position he was, to act as he did; far from the traditional story making Richard's life more intelligible, it would make it incomprehensible. Gairdner essays a battle between tradition and common sense with unconvincing results.

Leaving Dr Gairdner clinging to tradition in the face of all probability, we come to the present century and Sir Clements Markham's whole-hearted defence of Richard, *Richard III: His Life and Character*. Sir Clements is nothing if not single-minded; to him Richard is a combination of St George and Sir Galahad who never did an unworthy act in his life. This picture, though certainly more edifying than the traditional one, does not altogether carry conviction. Nobody was ever so noble and virtuous as Markham's Richard, certainly not a prince of the fifteenth century, when times were bloody and life cheap. If the Tudor Richard is too bad to be believed, Markham's is too good to be true. He is even exonerated of the killing of Hastings, for which he was undoubtedly to blame, whatever his excuse.

Markham's theory of the fate of the two children is ingenious and attractive but it fails for the same reason as the charge against Richard does – lack of evidence, though Henry certainly had the motive for the crime which Richard lacked. According to Markham, the murder was committed by Tyrell, but at Henry's command, not Richard's, and in the summer of 1486, not 1483. As proof he cites the curious fact that Tyrell received two general pardons from Henry, one in June and another a month later, in July 1486. Although this is an unusual occurrence, it is not unique, and there may be many reasons to account for it. Without any specific evidence it is pure guesswork to assert that the second pardon was given for murdering the boys during the month since Tyrell received the first.

The other piece of 'evidence' which Markham advances is that Elizabeth Woodville, who was then mother-in-law to Henry and had been restored by him to her royal rank and treated with much respect, was in February 1486/7 suddenly incarcerated[59] in the abbey at Bermondsey on a very flimsy pretext, the real reason being that she had begun to ask awkward questions as to the whereabouts of her sons. Again, there is no indication that this might have been the cause of her fall from favour. As the order for her incarceration was issued at the time of the Lambert Simnel rising and by the council which sat expressly to consider the measures to be taken to deal with it, it is evident that her offence was complicity in the rebellion.

From the point of view of both character and motive Henry is a far more likely murderer than Richard, and his subsequent treatment of the other surviving members of the Plantagenet family is a fair indication of the fate which Edward's two sons would have met had they come into his hands, but these are not sufficient reasons for so definite a statement as that he had the boys murdered in the Tower in the summer of 1486. If we assert lack of evidence in Richard's case we must also allow it in Henry's.

XII

SOME BONES

In 1674 workmen carrying out excavations on the south side of the White Tower in the Tower of London found, some ten feet deep in the ground under the foundations of a staircase leading from the then existing royal apartments to the Chapel of St John, some human bones. These were thrown on to a refuse heap, where they remained for an unspecified period until the news of their discovery came to the ears of Charles II, who gave orders that they should be collected and that Sir Christopher Wren should design a monument for their re-internment in Westminster Abbey. The wording of the commission to Wren was ' . . . that you provide a white marble coffin for the *supposed* bodies of the two princes' (*Sandford*; my italics), from which it is evident that King Charles was not prepared to commit himself beyond a certain point in his acceptance of the authenticity of the remains.

This is hardly surprising, for these were the third set of bones to be discovered in the Tower and endowed with royal rank. The first were said later to be those of a large ape which had escaped from the menagerie, climbed into an inaccessible and seldom visited turret, and had died there. The second set were found early in the seventeenth century behind the wall in a passage in the King's lodging, where a small room about seven or eight feet square was discovered (*Archaeologia*, vol. lxxxiv, p. 26, footnote). They were the bones of two children and were again immediately assumed to be those of the boys. Thus it will be seen that any bones which could by a stretch of the imagination be said to be those of children that have been found in the Tower since the days of Edward IV have automatically been assumed to be those of his missing sons. Doubtless there are plenty more awaiting discovery within the walls of that hoary haunt of evil, scene of so many tragedies.

However, after a further interval of four years, during which time little is known of their whereabouts except for a tradition that some of them found their way to the Ashmolean Museum, the bones were duly reburied in Sir Christopher's sarcophagus in Westminster Abbey, with an inscription in which their supposed unhappy owners are unequivocally stated to have been murdered by their uncle Richard III, though with no reference to any evidence which proves the allegation.

From this account, which is the accepted one, it will be seen that there are two gaps in the narrative during which the bones might have been lost and replaced, at least in part, with others, one being the possibly short time when they were on the rubbish heap after their first discovery, and the second a period of four years when they may have been anywhere, or even conceivably lost altogether. These two gaps in their history leave a considerable margin for reasonable doubts as to their identity before they had been subjected to any examination at all.

In 1933, after strong representations had been made to the authorities of Westminster Abbey, permission was given for their exhumation. They were duly exhumed on July 6th of that year and were examined by the late Professor W. Wright. Though examination did not take place in a properly equipped laboratory, but in the precincts of the Abbey itself, and while the tests available in such cases today were not available fifty-seven years ago, the report subsequently published in *Archaeologia* in 1934 by Dr L.E. Tanner, archivist of Westminster Abbey, and Professor Wright, is still quoted by many people, for no very adequate reason, as the last and incontrovertible word on the subject of Richard's guilt and must therefore be considered in any assessment of the evidence.

In his second paragraph Dr Tanner states that ' . . . the only two certain facts are, first, that from the day when Richard Duke of York joined his brother in the Tower of London neither of the brothers were ever seen again outside its walls; and secondly, that in 1674 some bones were found by chance under a staircase in the White Tower which were assumed to be those of the young princes and which were buried as such by Charles II's order in Henry VII's Chapel, Westminster Abbey.'

Even if the second point is conceded, though the casual treatment which the bones received after their initial discovery makes it at least debatable, the first 'fact' is an assumption for which there is no warrant whatever. It is *not* certain that the boys were never seen outside the Tower again. The most that can be asserted is that, so far as is known, there is no record of their having been seen, which is quite a different thing. Thus the basic premise of the report is open to question and nothing which subsequently emerges from it gives an adequate answer. Further on Dr Tanner refers again to the Tower 'from which neither of them ever emerged alive'. Once more he is assuming something which not only has never been proved but which has always been wide open to doubt.

He quotes Morton as being More's source of information, which he undoubtedly was, but then adds that 'he was in a position to know the facts'. This is very far from the truth, for Morton was either a prisoner or in exile during the relevant period and was in no position to know anything of the facts, though he was certainly in a position to distort or invent them afterwards. Here we are back at the old tainted source of evidence, which remains tainted however often it is quoted.

On a minor point Dr Tanner states in a footnote that 'it is most remarkable that on June 28th (1483) John Lord Howard was actually created Duke of York'. This is entirely incorrect. Howard was created *Duke of Norfolk*, a title to which he had a lineal claim but which had been held by Edward IV's younger son in right of his child-wife Ann Mowbray, who had died in infancy. The title of Duke of York was a royal one and it remained in abeyance during Richard's lifetime. It was not necessary for the boy to be dead for Richard to grant the title of Norfolk, to which he had such a slender claim, to someone else.[60] Such changes were at least as common among the noble families as they were in the rival royal houses, but that Dr Tanner should have made such an error of fact is not reassuring.

The late Professor Wright gives his report on the medical evidence. He finds that the bones are parts of the skeletons of two children of approximately $12\frac{1}{2}$ and 10 years of age, and of unknown sex, though he takes it for granted that they were boys. From certain dental similarities in the fragmentary jaws of the two skulls he deduces that the children were possibly related, though he admits that such evidence is difficult to obtain. The impression given is that he was determined to find it no matter what the difficulties. A red stain on the facial bones of the elder child is put down by Professor Wright to blood congested in the face as the result of suffocation, although he admits that he was unable to identify the nature of the stain, and a stain of this nature is often found in the case of natural death.[61]

As a result of these investigations we are left with the portions of two skeletons which are said to be those found under or near a staircase in the Tower, and which may – or may not – have been those of two boys of approximately the right ages, together with some rather flimsy evidence of possible relationship, and an unidentified stain. What in actual fact do these findings amount to?

In the first place there is nothing whatever to identify the remains as being those of any two particular children. They are simply some bones found in a fortress which has seen the deaths of innumerable unrecorded persons throughout its history. For centuries it was the royal palace as well as a fortress. It accommodated the whole court with all its servants, attendants, hangers-on and their families, who lived and often died within its walls, sometimes the victims of violence and sometimes of natural causes, such as the ever-recurring epidemics which raged in London until quite recent times. The bones may well be those of two children who died as the result of some such everyday tragedy. The fact that they were found under a staircase in accordance with the tradition begun by Tyrell's supposed confession is in itself a considerable measure of proof that they were not there in Henry's day, for he would have torn apart every staircase in the Tower until he was in a position to produce the pitiful evidence of Richard's revolting crime to a horrified world.

Instead of taking this obvious course Henry was at pains to invent the story of the mysterious priest who secretly reburied the bodies after Richard, having taken the double murder in his stride, boggled at the place of burial. This tale in its turn makes it impossible for the bones in question to be those of the boys. They are said to have been discovered buried ten feet deep under the foundations of the staircase, surely an impracticable task for a priest, or anyone else, to carry out alone and unobserved. This part of the story was invented by Henry for the express purpose of concealing the fact that there were no bodies to be discovered, and these particular bones were either there long before Henry's day and buried so deeply that he did not come upon them or they were not there at all and are those of two children of a later date.

The evidence as to age has been questioned by several later medical authorities in the light of modern techniques, and if

Professor Wright had not known the traditional story, would he have set so much importance on the very slender evidence of relationship, and would he not have put the unidentifiable 'blood-stain' down to what it probably was, a rust mark caused by contact with some piece of metal lying in the original grave with the bodies?

There is in fact nothing in the findings of the report that can help us in any way to solve the mystery; no proof of identity, no proof that the bodies were those of children of any particular century, no proof that a crime had been committed, or of how the bodies came to be buried where they were, or of how they died. They still remain some unidentified bones which lie among the Kings of England in Westminster Abbey. It will never be possible to establish their right to lie there.[62]

Dragon

his death, such as Fabyan and the writer of the *Great Chronicle of London* in England, and de Commines in France were either, as in the first case, pro-Lancastrian, or, as in the second, anti-English, and were further influenced by the Tudor line, which had become the official and generally accepted version within a few years of Bosworth. They were thus prejudiced and their evidence is correspondingly suspect. Later writers, such as Polydore Vergil and More, depend entirely on hearsay; in the case of Vergil the inspiration comes from Henry VII and in that of More from Morton, which practically rules them out of court. In every case 'common fame', in other words vulgar gossip, is the source quoted.

It will therefore be seen that the contemporary or near-contemporary chroniclers are of little value, and the only reliable sources of information are the records of the period, both public and private, of which a considerable number have survived, contrary to the generally accepted view. Among these are the record of Richard's legislation in the *Parliament Rolls*, references to him in municipal records, his grants in the *Patent Rolls*, and various miscellaneous documents relating to his household and his public departments. There are also a few revealing private letters which still survive and show a very different man to the monster of legend. Among the latter is a letter to his mother (*BL. Harl. MS. 433*) which goes far to prove that mother and son were very close to each other and to dispose of the story that Richard caused Shaw to slander the Duchess of York in his sermon at St Paul's Cross. In the same collection there is a letter to his Chancellor, the Bishop of Lincoln, written when his Solicitor General, Thomas Lynom, succumbed to the charms of the fair Jane Shore and wished to marry her, in spite of her complicity in the Hastings-Woodville plot and her subsequent disgrace. The letter is a model of tolerance and kindliness; far from forbidding the unwelcome match and ordering the disgrace of Lynom as he might well have done, the King merely asks the bishop to use his influence to stop it, adding that if Lynom is resolved he will give his consent, and in the meantime Jane is to be released and placed in the care of her father. Hardly the attitude of a tyrant.

There is also the letter now in the Public Record Office, written to the Chancellor at the time of Buckingham's rebellion, with a postscript in the King's own hand expressing his horror at his friend's treason and calling Buckingham 'the most untrue creature living', which he undoubtedly was. There is no trace of the cruel monster in any of these letters; indeed they are those of a gentle and honourable man and tell us more of the real Richard than anything else could possibly do. They are not official documents written with one eye on public opinion and the other on posterity.

His legislation shows consideration for his poorer subjects and a zeal for justice which benefitted the people while it lost the King powerful support. The civic records of York show the esteem and affection in which he was held by that city when he was Duke of Gloucester, and the touching entry in the council minutes recording his death is as fine an epitaph as any man could wish for: 'King Richard late mercifully reigning over us was through great treason . . . piteously slain and murdered, to the great heaviness of this city.' Brutal tyrants are not so mourned. The homely fact that he was known as 'Dickon' to his meanest subjects is in his favour, for men who are hated are not called by affectionate diminutives.

His loyalty to his brother was remarkable in that time of easy treasons. The only recorded occasion on which he opposed Edward was at the Treaty of Picquigny, when he alone refused the bribes of the King of France and spoke against what he considered to be a shameful betrayal of his country's interests and honour.[63]

Far from being the subtle schemer and 'deep dissembler' which later chroniclers accuse him of being, he had a great distaste for intrigue. He kept himself apart from the constant plottings which riddled Edward's court, going about his business in the north. Indeed, so little was he versed in intrigue that when he met it himself he was quite incapable of dealing with it. His own nature put him at a hopeless disadvantage with men like Buckingham, Hastings, and Stanley, to whom the atmosphere of plot and counter-plot was as natural as the air they breathed. They were incomprehensible to Richard as he was to them; each judged the other by his own standards until it was too late and tragedy was upon them all.

It is impossible for the most biassed anti-Ricardian to find any tenable charge that can be brought against Richard up to the time of Edward's death. He was a loyal and honourable man to whom his brother need feel no hesitation in committing the safety of his wife and children and the welfare of his country. Had that been all that Edward bequeathed to Richard the sequel would have been very different, but he was also leaving to his younger brother an impossible situation. From that unspoken bequest arose all the disasters of the next two years, culminating in Richard's own betrayal and death and the end of the House of York.

It is important to judge Richard's actions after Edward's death as we find them recorded at the time and without the embellishments of later writers, who, though they like to assume an inside knowledge of his motives, are in no position to tell us what went on in his mind.

Richard's actions on receiving the news of Edward's death away in the north were irreproachable. The ride to York with his train of mourners, the requiem mass and the public oath of allegiance to his nephew were both natural and fitting. There is no sign of indecent haste or impatience to ride south at speed and seize the reins of power. Even after receiving Hastings' news of what was going on in London he does not summon reinforcements but continues on his way with his small escort to meet his nephew at Northampton, and it is only here, after receiving further alarming news, that he takes the first strong measure to deal with the crisis brought about by the Woodvilles.

It is from now on that it becomes possible to put two diametrically opposed constructions on Richard's actions, the one honourable and the other base. The Tudor historians for their own reasons have chosen the latter; all Richard's acts are diabolical, his motives the very worst. In order to make their version at all consistent they have juggled with facts and dates, and where these have proved intractable they have not scrupled to fall back on sheer invention.

On the other hand Richard is entitled to be judged, in default of direct evidence, in the light of his own past record – the record of a man who for thirty years had shown himself loyal, honest and trustworthy. It is unlikely that such a man should almost overnight become false, double-dealing and perfidious. Evidence of character is all in Richard's favour and in its light the events of that summer of 1483 are at least comprehensible, whereas the Tudor version makes them improbable beyond the wildest imaginings.

Every act of Richard's till the middle of June is entirely consistent with an intention to crown his nephew. Not only is the boy treated with every respect as King and the preparations for his coronation speedily carried on, but the fact that Richard made no attempt to send for reinforcements seems conclusive proof that he was not contemplating any drastic change of the accepted plans. The shattering upheavals that took place between June 9th and 25th clearly indicate a crisis as unexpected as it was serious, and the urgent call to York for help on the 10th is not the action of a man who has been carefully plotting a *coup d'état* in his own favour, but rather of one who is suddenly confronted with a desperate and unexpected emergency.[64]

The whole incident of Shaw's clumsy sermon which was much more calculated to alarm the people than to allay their fears has an atmosphere of panic about it which is very foreign to Richard's character but may well have reflected the feeling of the Council, faced with the problem of an illegitimate heir, Woodville plots, an uneasy country, and the threat of civil disturbances. It is not surprising if the citizens, frightened and bewildered by these sudden changes which they did not understand, were at first reluctant to commit themselves and became the prey of inspired rumour. Who should blame them? It was only when Richard had finally accepted the crown and had taken his seat on the King's Bench in Westminster Hall that the common people felt it safe to acclaim him, but when it came, their approbation was whole-hearted, and throughout the coronation celebrations there is no hint of there having been unrest or dissatisfaction.

Richard's real motives in accepting the crown remain buried in his own heart, as he has left no personal record which could supply a clue to his thoughts. They were probably, as is usually the case, mixed, but it is certain that he capitulated to the urgent demands of the leading men of the country, and it is equally certain that by so doing he saved it from a renewed outbreak of civil war. He was no more a usurper than his brother Edward had been, and neither then nor at any later time had he cause to fear that his title, confirmed by the *Titulus Regius*, could with reason or legality be called in question. He had therefore no reason to wish his nephews dead. On the contrary, their continued existence was a safeguard against an attempt on the throne by Henry Tudor, the only potential pretender, through marriage with the boys' sister.

It is significant that the only public reference to their supposed murder comes from the Continent, when, in January of 1483/4 the French Chancellor, in a speech to the Etats-Généraux, accuses Richard of having had them put to death. His inspiration probably came from Mancini's gossip, for Mancini was a friend of the Chancellor. Morton had also arrived in France shortly before. *The Great Chronicle of London* records that after Easter 1484 there was 'much whispering among the people that the King had put the children of Edward IV to death'. Thus it will be seen that the stories were current in France sometime before they were at all general in England, and it is not difficult to trace their source to Henry Tudor and his advisers.

Rastell in his *Pastyme of Peoples* tells of a variety of stories which went the rounds as to the fate of the boys, thus proving that nothing was known and that the various stories were nothing but tittle-tattle. The secrecy in which the whole affair was wrapped is in itself proof that Richard was not their murderer. If for any reason he had decided that their deaths were necessary he would have had to give out some explanation of their fate, for obviously a secret murder would defeat its own ends. If it was expedient that they should die, it was equally expedient that they should be known beyond all shadow of doubt to be dead.

Richard's only course would have been to let them be seen to be well treated until speculation as to their future had died down, then arrange a murder which would look like a natural death – not a difficult task in those days of epidemics and little medical knowledge – followed by an exposure of the bodies at St Paul's and a funeral befitting their father's sons. Richard could have picked his own time for the murder and if he had been what the Tudors made him out to be, cruel, deceitful, a 'deep dissimular', this is what he would have done. The one thing he could not afford was a secret crime, followed by a mystery, at a time when there had been considerable speculation as to the future fate of the children, and at the beginning of what there was every reason to suppose would be a long reign.

It is impossible to say with certainty that any person is incapable of murder. In the history of crime the most unlikely people have committed the most improbable homicides. Given a sufficient motive, enough courage, and the opportunity, we are all potential murderers; but if ever there was a man of whom it could be said, having regard to the circumstances and all the reliable evidence we have as to his personal record and character, 'this man is incapable of this crime', then that man is Richard III, and the crime is the quite pointless and incredibly stupid murder of his nephews. There is no single factor which could account for his guilt; no motive, nothing in his previous character or in his subsequent treatment of others.

Yet it is not any of these things which speak loudest in his favour, nor even the implied testimony of Elizabeth Woodville's confidence in him six months after he was supposed to have murdered her sons. Richard's strongest advocate is Henry Tudor himself. Henry Tudor, who worked so hard to blacken the name of the man he had supplanted; Henry Tudor, who suppressed the *Titulus Regius* because he dared not remind the world of the validity of Richard's claim; Henry Tudor, who has by his own tortuous schemings, gradually revealed, provided the strongest proof of Richard's innocence.

If Richard was guilty, why no accusation in the Act of Attainder? Why no solemn requiem mass for the dead children at a time when these pious exercises were considered of such importance, and which would surely have been ordered by Henry from policy or by his Queen as a family duty to her brothers? Why did it take Henry twenty years and a faked posthumous confession to establish a story whose main outlines he must have discovered within twenty-four hours of taking possession of the Tower had there been a word of truth in it? Why all those years of anxiety over pretenders to the throne if proof of their impostures lay ready to his hand?

How is it possible that in all that time he could gain no clue to the mystery if the story which he ultimately gave out had been true? No word of the taking over of the Tower for one night by Tyrell, coinciding with the disappearance of the children, and no hint of the reburial by the priest who could not have carried out his task alone and in complete secrecy. If, on the other hand, the bodies were lying all the time under the staircase where they were originally supposed to have been buried, why did Henry not find them when he made 'diligent search'? And why was Tyrell not tried on a charge of murder and regicide instead of being hastily executed on a minor charge before his 'confession' was made public?[65] That Henry had to make use of such a ridiculous story to bring about a result which he had ardently desired for so long is the best possible proof that he was unable after years of trying to find any grounds at all for his accusation.

In English law a person is innocent until he is proved guilty – not merely asserted or supposed to be guilty on prejudiced evidence. In the matter of Richard III and the supposed death of his nephews there is no case to bring before the court at all. It should be dismissed from the bar of history.

Richard's whole reign, short as it was, clearly shows that he intended to rule with justice and mercy. The liberal reforms which he sponsored in his one parliament are an indication of what he might have done had he been given time. His treatment of both friend and foe was noticeable for its generosity. After Buckingham's rebellion there were few executions and he showed great, and in the event, misplaced leniency towards Lady Stanley and innumerable lesser offenders.

The reason for his failure and his downfall lay in the fact that he was no politician, and that he had no sense of expediency or of timing. His goal was what he held to be right and he aimed straight for it regardless of the enemies he might make on the way. Honesty and straightforwardness, the very qualities which had brought him success as a soldier and an administrator, were responsible for losing him the support of the powerful men of his kingdom, who found their own interests to be in direct conflict with their King's determination to 'use his authority and office as he ought' (*Buck, Vergil*).

Nevertheless, he might have weathered all storms had it not been for the devastating blow he sustained in the loss of his only son and heir, a blow which left him a broken man and the kingdom in the desperate hazard of an unsecured succession, and which together with Richard's own fatal tendency to place his trust in traitors, gave to Henry Tudor, his scheming mother, and a handful of treacherous nobles their chance to take the road which led to the tragic disaster of Bosworth field.

The only stain on Richard's memory remains the execution of his false friend Hastings. Of the many thousand words written about him, the fairest and most balanced summing up is that of Thomas Carte:

> Facts, and the general tenor of a man's conduct best show his real character, and all the virulent and atrocious calumnies founded purely on surmises, a perverse imagination, or downright false-hood, and thrown upon Richard by the flatterers of his successor whose cruelty came by that means to be overlooked, will never efface the just praise due to Richard for his excellent laws and his constant application to see justice impartially distributed and good order established in all parts of England.

XIV

NO MURDER IN THE TOWER

*W*hat *did* happen to Edward IV's sons?

The mystery which surrounds their ultimate fate has proved fascinating to successive generations of the learned and the ignorant alike and no conclusive proof has ever come to light which could provide a solution that did no rest solely on speculation. The possibilities are endless, but all remain at best quite unsupported theories.

There were three main groups of people who had an interest, for widely differing motives, in the boys. There was the King himself and his followers, there was Elizabeth Woodville and her supporters, and lastly there was Henry Tudor and the remnant of the old Lancastrian party. To each group the children were of the greatest importance, with this distinction, that in the case of the first two it was important that they should survive, whereas in the case of Henry Tudor their deaths were essential to the validity of his claim to the throne through his intended wife, their sister, which, however distasteful it may have been to Henry, was the chief reason for the support he received in the early stages of his invasion plans and for his final acceptance by the country.

Henry therefore had the real compelling motive for their removal, and Buck in his *History of Richard III* makes the statement, which he does not substantiate, that 'an old manuscript book which I have seen says that Doctor Morton and a certain countess, contriving the death of Edward V and others, resolved it by poison'. The 'certain countess' would seem to be Lady Stanley, mother of Henry Tudor, who is often referred to by her earlier title of Countess of Richmond and who had every reason to wish Elizabeth of York's brothers out of the way to clear the road to the throne for Henry and their sister. Her husband held a high position at court, and as the Duke of Buckingham, who within a month of Richard's coronation was deeply involved with her and Dr Morton, was Lord High Constable, there would have been little difficulty in getting access to the boys and in doing away with them, particularly if the method used was poison. Buckingham himself has been put forward as the possible murderer, and certainly his unstable character does not speak in his favour. There also remains Markham's theory, which accuses Henry himself, on very slender evidence, of having had them killed in the summer of 1486 by Sir James Tyrell.

There is, however, one insuperable obstacle to bringing a serious charge against either Henry or any of his supporters. *Had anyone connected with him been the murderer he must have known about it.* He would have been in no sort of doubt that the boys were dead and he would have been free to make out his own convincing case against Richard, enforced with a definite and damning accusation in the Act of Attainder of November 1485. He could easily have produced two bodies of approximately the right ages together with witnesses who, real or false, would not have been lacking, for the disappearance of the children could not have gone unnoticed in the Tower at least. He would thus have proved to the world that there were no male Plantagenets, except the feeble-minded Warwick in the Tower, left to threaten his throne and his dynasty.

It is quite evident from his own actions that Henry did *not* know, and was never able to find out, what had happened to the boys, and he was haunted by the fear that they might still be alive and reappear to give the lie to his accusations and to claim the throne. He knew that Lambert Simnel certainly and Perkin Warbeck probably were imposters, but what *had* happened to the sons of Edward IV was a mystery which he was never able to solve. For twenty years Henry hinted and whispered, lied and slandered, until he felt it safe to bring his accusations into the open with a false confession and Sir James Tyrell as scapegoat.

What of Elizabeth Woodville? Apart from her natural feelings as a mother, her two sons were her chief hope of gaining power for herself, and such a hope must have died hard in a woman of her ambitious temperament. If she could regain possession of one or both of the boys and remove them overseas to some secret place of safety she would have gone to any length to attain this aim. Kidnapping two boys from the Tower would seem to be a hopeless enterprise, but we have after all no reason to believe that they remained in the Tower, neither for that matter do we know what secret supporters Elizabeth Woodville had in high places. It is at least a possibility which cannot be ruled out.

Finally we come to Richard himself. He had no motive to kill the boys. They had been declared illegitimate and removed from the succession by general consent of the country's leading citizens, not to please the Duke of Gloucester but because nobody wanted a minor, and a Woodville minor at that, as King. Even if they died there remained their five sisters, whose 'claims' were at least as good as theirs, and the Duke of Clarence's son, Warwick, who was only debarred from the succession by his father's attainder, which could at any time have been reversed. Most people in those days, including Richard himself, had come under the ban of attainder at some time during their lives, so that if there was any threat to Richard's crown it lay in young Warwick, whom he treated with the greatest kindness, as he did his nieces.

There was, however, a far more positive reason why the survival of his nephews should have been of the utmost importance to him. The events of the weeks immediately preceding his coronation had very naturally produced a luxuriant crop of dark rumours concerning Richard's intentions. Richard showed himself to be very sensible of this dangerous atmosphere, and very sensitive to it, in his reluctance, recorded by friend and foe alike, to accept the crown under such inauspicious circumstances.

Such talk was inevitable then and would be inevitable in similar circumstances at any time, but no man in Richard's position could afford to ignore it. Still less could he afford to justify it by murdering the children within a matter of weeks. Even had he been the monster of legend, he would have had, for his own sake, to avoid that particular crime until popular misgivings had had time to die down. Whatever happened, the two children needed to be preserved, because if anything happened to them, for whatever cause, it was their uncle who would bear the responsibility. To put it on the lowest plane, self-interest must have kept the sons of Edward IV safe from their uncle, Richard III.

It is extremely probable that they did not remain in the Tower for long, and that Richard had them removed secretly to some safe place in the country where they could no longer be used as the focus of further Woodville plots, of which Richard had had more than enough experience, and which he would have regarded as a continued menace to the peace of the country. It is very possible that the news of the fomented agitations to 'deliver' them and of the 'meetings and confederacies' being held in the southern counties with the same object reached him during his progress to the north, and that he sent Sir James Tyrell back to London, not to murder them, but to remove them from their undesirable proximity to their mother, in sanctuary at Westminster.

It is also possible that Elizabeth Woodville did afterwards manage to get possession of them and smuggle them out of the country, but too late to help her ambitions, for by that time it was Henry Tudor who had rallied the malcontents to his own banner with the attractive promise of the marriage of the red and white roses and an end to civil dissension. Or both children may have died natural deaths, the victims of one of the constant epidemics which swept all parts of the country at that time. Or they may have simply disappeared, in the turmoil of those troubled days. Then there is the mysterious 'Plantagenet' who lived in obscurity at Eastwell in Kent, where he earned his living as a bricklayer until his death in 1550. Legend has it that he was an illegitimate son of Richard's, but Richard had two illegitimate children whom he recognized: why should he have been so secretive about a third, and is it not at least as likely that the mysterious bricklayer was really one of his nephews, who wisely preferred a life of obscurity to the certainty of an early demise under the Tudors?

It will thus be seen that the whole question of the fate of the 'princes in the Tower' remains an open one, with the weight of evidence on the survival of one or both of them for an unknown number of years, though it would also seem that at the time of Bosworth their whereabouts may have been unknown to Richard as well as Henry, or it is difficult to account for his failure to produce them and so destroy Henry's main asset – his proposed marriage to their sister. On the other hand, there may well have been urgent reasons, of which we have no record, why to keep their hiding place a secret was for Richard the lesser of two evils, particularly if it was in any case known to members of his inner council, as it doubtless would have been. If this was so, it is possible that Richard himself had them sent overseas, knowing that their lives would be in danger if Henry's invasion proved successful, as it did. Such a step would have been quite in keeping with Richard's sense of duty; if circumstances and the ambition of their maternal relatives had made it impossible for him to secure the throne for his brother's sons he could at least fulfil part of his trust and secure their lives.

Unless and until some further evidence of a reliable nature comes to light, the whole mystery must remain insoluble. So far there is not sufficient proof to bring a murder charge against anybody, or indeed to assume that a murder was ever committed at all.

Boar Badge

NOTES

1. This strange rumour was reported in 1461 to the Duke of Milan, 'although they say his Majesty remarked at another time, that he must be the son of the Holy Spirit etc' (*Calendar of Milanese State Papers*, 1912, p. 58). There is no doubt that rumours to the effect that Edward was not Henry's son did circulate from at least 1456, but there is equally no doubt that Henry was well aware that Margaret was pregnant, nor of his joy at the birth when he recovered from his mental attack at Christmas 1454 (*Henry VI*, R.A. Griffiths, 1981, pp. 717, 719, and references there cited). Henry's incapacity to rule had undoubtedly increased after his illness.

2. There are several other sources showing the contemporary belief that Edward was killed in battle. The growth of the legend of his murder is most interesting. See Appendix 2, 'The Death of Edward of Lancaster', in P.W. Hammond, *The Battles of Barnet and Tewkesbury*, 1990, pp. 123–6. The *Fleetwood Chronicle* is now more frequently called *The Arrivall*.

3. John of Gaunt married his mistress, Katherine Swinford, after the death of his second wife, and their children were legitimated, firstly by the Pope, and then by Richard II, their cousin. Richard issued Letters Patent on 9 February 1397, on the same day having them read in parliament and approved by those present. The version in the Rolls of Parliament stated that it was in the words of the Patent, and said unequivocally that 'you be able to be . . . admitted to any kind of honours, dignities, pre-eminences . . . by whatever name they be called', i.e. with no restrictions on inheriting the throne. There is thus no doubt that, in effect, a statute was passed legitimizing the Beauforts without qualification. The ambiguity arises because in the reign of Henry IV the Patent was re-issued to the eldest Beaufort, purportedly in the words of the original, but which, however, added between the words 'dignities' and 'pre-eminences', 'except the royal dignity'. Reference to the 1397 Patent Roll itself shows that these words, not originally there, had been added at a different time in a different hand. This addition, in the absence of a new statute can have had no legally binding effect whatever, but was obviously an attempt on the part of Henry IV to remove his step-brothers and -sister from the succession in order to avoid any possible clash between them and his sons or descendants. See 'The Beaufort Legitimation' in M.H. Jackson-Lipkin, *Coat of Arms*, vol. 4, 1956–58, pp. 321–328. James Gairdner in his *Richard III*, 1898, pp. 107–8, discusses the problem briefly.

4. Edward raised much of the money needed by means of grants of taxation by parliament, but topped it up by means of these forced gifts. See C.L. Scofield, *The Life and Reign of Edward IV*, vol. 2, 1923, pp. 44–5, 48, 94–5, for benevolences see pp. 104–5.

5. It appears that Gloucester was one of several of Edward's councillors who opposed the peace. Commines says: 'The duke of Gloucester, the King of England's brother, and several others, who were not pleased by this peace, were not present at the conference [between Edward IV and Louis XI]. But later they reconciled themselves to it, and shortly afterwards the duke of Gloucester came to visit the King [Louis XI] at Amiens and the King gave him some very fine presents, including plate and well equipped horses.' (Phillippe de Commines, *Memoirs*, translated by Michael Jones, 1972, p. 259). For the presents given to Edward's other councillors, see Scofield, vol. 2, pp. 146–7. See also note 62.

6. A considerable amount is now known about 'Jane' Shore, whose real name was Elizabeth. Her father was John Lambert, a prominent mercer of London, her first husband was William Shore, another mercer. She was first named Jane by Thomas Heywood in his play *King Edward the Fourth*, published in 1599. See Nicholas Barker, 'Jane Shore: Part I, The Real Jane Shore' and Sir Robert Birley, 'Jane Shore: Part II, Jane Shore in Literature', *Etoniana*, no. 125, 4 June 1972, pp. 383–91, 391–7, and no. 126, 2 December 1972, pp. 399–407. Part II of this article shows how 'Elizabeth' came to be 'Jane'.

7. For the education and household of the future Edward V, see Nicholas Orme, 'The Education of Edward V', *Bulletin of the Institute of Historical Research*, vol. 57, 1984, pp. 119–30. This article prints the regulations for the household and demonstrates the extent of the Woodville influence.

8. The problem of whether or not Edward left a second will which appointed Richard of Gloucester as Protector is insoluble, short of finding it. It seems very likely that there was such a document. The only will known, of 1475, is printed in *Excerpta Historica*, 1831, pp. 366–79. For remarks on the possibility of a second will, see *ibid*, p. 366, and on the appointment of Richard as Protector see Charles Ross, *Richard III*, 1981, pp. 40–1. See also Polydore Vergil, *English History*, ed. Henry Ellis, Camden Society, 1844, p. 173.

9. Edward's brother George was created Duke of Clarence on 28 June 1461, and Richard was created Duke of Gloucester on 1 November 1461. George was nominated Knight of the Garter in 1461, Richard sometime before February 1466, see respective entries in G.E. Cokayne, *The Complete Peerage*.

10. The *Historie of the Arrivall of Edward IV in England*, the most reliable source for this event, says that a group headed by King Edward rode to meet George of Clarence at Banbury. The group included the Duke of Gloucester. This also says that the Dukes of Clarence and Gloucester spoke privately after King Edward had embraced and forgiven Clarence. There is no doubt that Clarence

came to Banbury intending to change sides. See *Battles of Barnet and Tewkesbury*, p. 64.

11. Warwick and Montagu were never formally attainted and deprived of their estates, but it is possible to argue that by appearing in arms against the King with banners displayed, they commited manifest treason. The King himself being present, the crime needed no other proof, and they thereby forfeited all their goods. However, it was usual by this period to attaint traitors by parliamentary act, thus avoiding any question of legal flaw in the process. Neither Warwick nor Montagu were ever attainted in this manner, but their lands were undoubtedly treated as forfeit in that they were granted away to Clarence and Gloucester in due course. The delay and lack of formal attainder was probably due to the complex political situation between Clarence, married to one of Warwick's heiresses, and Gloucester, who wished to marry the other. The final division of lands was a mixture of grants of forfeited lands, and the anticipation of hereditary right (of lands legally belonging to the Countess of Warwick). The complicated legal situation is dealt with in J.G. Bellamy, *The Law of Treason in England in the later Middle Ages*, 1970, pp. 192–3, 201–2; for the equally complicated political situation see M.A. Hicks, 'Descent, Partition and Extinction: the "Warwick Inheritance"', *Bulletin of the Institute of Historical Research*, vol. 52, 1979, pp 116–28. There is no reason to doubt the affection between Anne and Richard of Gloucester.

12. It is not certain which of the two Dukes, Clarence or Gloucester, received the largest share of the estates. See the article by M.A. Hicks cited in note 11.

13. The 'Council of the North' at this period (as said here, virtually the Council of the Duke) probably met at Middleham or Sheriff Hutton, castles owned by the Duke.

14. Hastings was reported as having sent letters to Richard (Mancini, *The Usurpation of Richard III*, 1969, pp. 70–3, Vergil, p. 173), and Buckingham must also have done so, although we have no evidence. The arrangements to meet would have ensured an exchange of letters.

15. The letters which it is known that Ratcliffe carried to York and Lord Neville, nephew of the Earl of Westmorland (both printed in P.M. Kendall, *Richard III*, 1487 (Anne F. Sutton, 'The Hautes of Kent', *The Ricardian*, vol. 6, 1982, p.55). Haute and Vaughan. It is possible that Ratcliffe carried such instructions, as the timing could fit. He reached York on June 15, and Rivers knew that he would die by 23 June (for his will, dated then, see *Excerpta Historica*, pp. 246–8). He was executed on 25 June. Haute may have been held in the north after his arrest at Northampton; he was not executed, however, and died on Palm Sunday 1487 (Anne F. Sutton, 'The Hautes of Kent', *The Ricardian*, vol. 6, 1982, p. 55.

16. More is reporting a conversation here between Edward and his mother. The word 'bigamy' is being used in the sense of a marriage with a woman who had been married before. See discussion in Thomas More, *The History of King Richard III*, ed. R.S. Sylvester, 1963, pp. 241–2.

17. For Haute see note 15.

18. Edward of Middleham was knighted a few days after the welcome in a
     ceremony organized by Richard, at which he first invested his son as Prince of
     Wales (see *British Library Harleian Manuscript 433*, ed. Rosemary Horrox and
     P.W. Hammond, vol. 1, 1979, p. 2, and *The Crowland Chronicle Continuations
     1459–1486*, ed. Nicholas Pronay and John Cox, 1986, pp. 160, 161). The
     ceremony was not of course a second coronation as stated by Crowland.

19. It is perhaps unlikely that Richard would have contemplated the execution of
     Lady Stanley, although he went to the length of having an act passed against
     her in which the 'great punishment of attainder' was remitted, and all her lands
     given to her husband for his life (*Rolls of Parliament*, vol. 6, p. 250).

20. The Woodville and Stanley following could be described as ex-Yorkist, as
     were the members of Edward IV's household, many of whom, recent work
     has shown, fled to Brittany following the collapse of the Buckingham
     rebellion. See, for example, Rosemary Horrox, *Richard III: a study of service*,
     1989, pp. 273–94, particularly pp. 275 *ff*. These pages show the part played
     by former supporters of Edward IV (among others) in the downfall of
     Richard III.

21. In a sense the stories did attain a higher status than gossip since they formed the
     foundation of the accusations against Richard written by the later chroniclers.

22. These two quotations from the *Rolls of Parliament* come from vol. 6, pp. 240
     and 289. The act of Henry VII does in fact go so far as to order the removal of
     Richard's *Titulus Regius* from the 'Roll and Records of the said Parliament'.
     Since it was not, we can now quote it as above. The *Rolls of Parliament* (final
     versions rather than drafts), were among the documents stored in the Tower.
     Interestingly, the Lords in parliament wished to examine Bishop Stillington,
     author of the 'false bill', but Henry refused to allow this, saying he had
     pardoned him and did not wish to proceed against him (S.B. Chrimes, *English
     Constitutional Ideas in the Fifteenth Century*, 1936, p. 266, note 4).

23. It is undoubtedly true that Henry was here bringing forward all possible
     charges against Richard. It is also true, though, that in the relatively few
     fifteenth-century acts of attainder the wording is not uniform. The words
     'shedding of infants blood' are not conventional in this context, but if Henry
     was here referring to the deaths of the Princes one wonders why he should use
     a phrase so vague as to be virtually meaningless.

24. It is also true to say, of course, that there is no actual record of requiem masses
     for the deaths of many who died violent deaths at this time.

25. Interestingly, the Duke of York and Earl of Salisbury announced (untruly) the
     death of Henry VI before the 'battle' of Ludford in 1459 and had a requiem said
     (*Rolls of Parliament*, vol. 5, p. 348).

26. This was Margaret of York, dowager Duchess of Burgundy, sister of Edward IV and Richard III.

27. We do not of course know for certain whether or not Elizabeth Woodville's residence at Bermondsey Abbey was voluntary or the result of a more or less forceful suggestion by Henry VII, but it is undoubtedly true that the King transferred all her lands and annuities to her daughter. The Privy Seal writ announcing the transfer merely says that for 'diverse considerations' the lands and annuities had been 'assigned unto our dearest wife and Queen' (*Materials for a History of the Reign of Henry VII*, ed. William Campbell, Rolls Series, 1877, vol. 2, p. 148). The writ does not say that Elizabeth Woodville had resigned the lands due to her desire to retire to the convent, which one might have expected if this had been the case. Bacon is the sole source for the statement that Henry condemned Elizabeth Woodville for making her peace with Richard III. However, Henry did not subsequently behave in a vindictive fashion towards her, but rather made gifts to her on various occasions between 1488 and her death, and an annuity of £400 per annum in February 1490 (David MacGibbon, *Elizabeth Woodville*, 1938, p. 196, see also pp. 192–5 and references, especially to her appearances at court after 1487, given there and in S.B. Chrimes, *Henry VII*, p. 76, note 3). Henry may well have been taking precautions in 1487, suspecting an involvement with the Lambert Simnel uprising. His action may also perhaps have been connected with rumours that one of the sons of Edward IV was alive. For recent comments see Michael Bennett, *Lambert Simnel and the Battle of Stoke*, 1987, pp. 50–1.

28. See note 26 for Elizabeth Woodville's involvement with Simnel.

29. It might be proposed that William Shakespeare was, in this context, one of the finest propagandists who ever lived, see chapter X below. For Morton as propagandist author of More's *Richard III*, see note 48.

30. It is perhaps now more frequently referred to as the Rous Roll.

31. Edward of Lancaster was also added, as first husband of Anne Neville. For a full description of both versions see A.R. Wagner, *A Catalogue of English Medieval Rolls of Arms*, 1950, pp. 116–20. The English version was reprinted as *The Rous Roll* by John Rous, in 1980, with an introduction by Charles Ross.

32. For Rous' only reference to Richard's shoulders see next page and note 33.

33. Rous' description of Richard, apart from his appearance at birth, with 'teeth and hair to his houlders', runs: 'He was small of stature, with a short face and unequal shoulders, the right higher and the left lower.' See Alison Hanham *Richard III and his early historians 1483–1535*, 1975, pp. 120, 121 (in a complete translation of this part of the *Historia*).

34. For Morton's part in the development of the legend, see note 48.

35. Fabyan was the first *English* chronicler to suggest that Edward of Lancaster was murdered after Tewkesbury. Fabyan was writing in about 1504. The first chroniclers to refer to the 'murder' were continental, writing as soon as 1473. See reference in note 2.

36. The dating of the records of these various rumours is difficult. It now seems probable that Rous in his *Historia Regum Angliae*, now dated to about 1490, was the first to directly accuse Richard of the murder. For a full discussion of the rumours, see W.J. White, 'The Death and Burial of Henry VI, A Review of the facts and theories: Part I', *The Ricardian*, vol. 6, 1982, pp. 70–80.

37. Perhaps relative poverty, in view of the comments in note 27.

38. Recent work shows that the Spaniards refused to seal the alliance, rather than to consider it, while Warwick and Warbeck were alive. The whole situation is rather confused, see Chrimes, *Henry VII*, p. 284, note 8 and references there.

39. The position of Tyrell during the reign of Henry VII seems to have been a rather ambiguous one. He undoubtedly lost control of all his Welsh and border lands, wardships, offices and fees at the beginning of the reign, although whether by design or not is unclear. In February 1488 he was, however, granted compensation in Guisnes for his losses (which he estimated at £3,011), and his Welsh lands, etc., were taken into the hands of the King (see *Calendar of Patent Rolls 1485–1494*, 1914, pp. 216–18, for a list of the lands, etc.). He was re-appointed Sheriff of Glamorgan and Constable of Cardiff Castle in February 1486 (as from Michaelmas 1485), and remained Lieutenant of Guisnes. He seems to have remained chiefly at Guisnes for the rest of his life, although he attended some Court ceremonies, which suggests that Henry was keeping him at arms length. See *History of Parliament, Biographies 1439–1509*, ed. J.C. Wedgwood, 1936, pp. 889–90, and *Dictionary of National Biography*.

40. Whether or not Henry VII 'gave out' that Tyrell confessed to the murder is discussed by Susan Leas in 'As the King Gave out', *The Ricardian*, vol. 4, no. 56, 1977, pp. 2–4.

41. For a discussion of the charges that Vergil destroyed records, see Denys Hay, *Polydore Vergil, Renaissance Historian and Man of Letters*, 1952, pp. 157–60, particularly pp. 159–60. Hay does not credit the charges.

42. For Haute, see note 15.

43. 'Signed', in general in the sense of being issued in the name of the king.

44. For Haute, see note 15.

45. Vergil undoubtedly consulted original documents in the course of his work, including the statutes, but since this was chiefly (if not entirely) from printed sources, it seems quite likely that he knew nothing of *Titulus Regius* in its

manuscript form, though it seems probable that he had heard of it. This would make his description of events even more odd. The quotations from Vergil on this page are from pp. 184 and 187. For Vergil's use of sources, see Hay, pp. 87–9.

46. Records of medieval coronations are generally rather poor, that of Richard III happens to be one of the best documented (see Anne F. Sutton and P.W. Hammond, *The Coronation of Richard III: the extant documents*, 1983). Richard's coronation was certainly well attended and was as far as possible from a 'scratch affair', but it is difficult to compare it with others.

47. For recent discussions of Vergil's work see chapters 4 and 5 of Hay's book (note 41), and chapter 6 of Hanham's book (note 33).

48. The continuation was by Richard Grafton. The possible involvement of Morton with More's *History* is discussed by Richard Sylvester in his edition of *The History of King Richard III*, pp. lix–lxiii. Sylvester agrees that much of More's information probably came from Morton. For Grafton's involvement, see Sylvester, pp. 273–6. Morton's part in anti-Ricardian propaganda is not quite as clear.

49. As noted in note 47, the continuator of Hardyng was Grafton.

50. 'Potter' was probably Richard Potter, who became Attorney in Chancery. 'Mistlebrook' was probably William Mistlebrook, who was auditor of various Crown lands to both Richard III and Henry VII. He may well have known Potter therefore, (Sylvester, p. 170). Both would thus know something of recent events, but not necessarily a great deal.

51. It is perhaps more likely that More would know Vergil's work rather than that of Rous, which was not published until 1716. Vergil was writing at about the same time as More.

52. See note 22.

53. More of course was writing a 'tragedy', and may not have regarded *Titulus Regius* as very relevant to his purposes, but Vergil may well have known of the Act (see note 44) and if so it is difficult to believe that Hall and Grafton did not know of it.

54. Grafton in Hardyng, see note 48.

55. At the death of Henry VII there remained of the children of John de la Pole Duke of Suffolk and Elizabeth, his wife (and sister of Edward IV and Richard III): the eldest, Edmund Earl of Suffolk; Edmund's daughter Anne, a nun; Richard (died 1525), later calling himself Duke of Suffolk and known as the 'White Rose'; William (died 1539); possibly Humphrey, a priest; and perhaps one of the two, three, or four daughters.

56. That is, the enrolled version on the Parliament Rolls, perhaps overlooked as much as forgotten.

57. This treatise, also known as *The Encomium of Richard III*, was in the form of a paradox, i.e. an example of a late sixteenth/early seventeenth century genre, in defence or praise of something generally regarded as indefensible, such as debt or sadness. There is some evidence that in this case the author was in fact serious about his defence. See Sir William Cornwallis the Younger, *The Encomium of Richard III*, ed. A.N. Kincaid, 1977.

58. Sir George Buck's account of his ancestor seems to owe more to family piety than accuracy. There is no record of this ancestor as a household official of Richard III, nor of his being a knight. He was attainted after Bosworth, but as plain 'John Buck' (*Rolls of Parliament*, vol. 6, p. 276). See George Buck, *The History of King Richard the Third*, ed. A.N. Kincaid, 1979, pp. xiii, cvii–cviii, 260, for a discussion of John Buck.

59. Possibly 'relegated' rather than 'incarcerated', see note 27.

60. There has been much discussion of this question, see for example Anne Crawford, 'The Mowbray Inheritance' in *Richard III: Crown and People*, ed. J.O. Petre, 1985, p. 83, where it is argued that it was illegal for Richard to grant the Norfolk title to another person without first removing it from Richard of York. There has apparently been none by Peerage lawyers. One recent general opinion is that titles of honour cannot be abrogated except by clear and precise words in an Act of Parliament (R.P. Gadd, *Peerage Law*, 1985, pp. 102, 122). Peerage law was not precisely formulated in the fifteenth century, though, and it is quite possible that Richard III felt himself perfectly entitled to overrule a title granted by charter by a charter of his own.

61. Staining of bones is very rarely due to events during death; it is certainly extremely unlikely to be blood-staining. For a recent discussion of these bones see P.W. Hammond and W.J. White, 'The Sons of Edward IV: A Re-examination of the Evidence on their Deaths and on the Bones in Westminster Abbey' in *Richard III: Loyalty Lordship and Law*, ed. P.W. Hammond, 1986, pp. 104–47.

62. Recent work has shown that it is now possible to recover genetic information from ancient skeletal material (Erika Hagelberg et al., 'Ancient Bone DNA Amplified', *Nature*, vol. 342, 1989, p. 485), which might one day make it possible to compare the bones from Westminster Abbey with those of Edward IV in order to settle finally (perhaps) the question of relationship. Other recent methods for relating and ageing) bones are discussed in the reference in note 61.

63. See note 5. The presents which Louis XI gave to Edward's councillors would not necessarily be regarded as bribes, either by Louis or the recipients, but as a just recognition of status.

64. There is no doubt that an emergency of some kind had arisen at about this time, but it must have been one that Richard thought he could contain for a short while at least from other resources since help from York could not have arrived in less than ten days at best. In fact it arrived on 3 July (Sutton and Hammond, p. 27). It is possible that Richard also asked for help from other areas, as hinted at in Mancini, and that these arrived earlier (Mancini, pp. 99, 100).

65. Tyrell was tried and afterwards executed on a charge of 'falsely and traitorously imagining the death and destruction of the King our Sovereign lord, and the subversion of this his Realm', (Roll of Parliament, vol. 6, p. 545).

BIBLIOGRAPHY

PART ONE: BOOKS USED BY THE AUTHOR

CONTEMPORARY SOURCES

British Library Harleian Manuscript 433.

Commines, Philippe de, *The Memoirs*, ed. Andrew Scoble, 2 vols, London, 1911.

Calendar of the Patent Rolls, Edward IV, Henry VI, 1467–1477, London, 1900.

Calendar of the Patent Rolls, Edward IV–Richard III, 1476–1485, London, 1901.

Cely Papers, ed. H.E. Malden, Camden Society, 1900.

Child, F.J., *The English and Scotch Popular Ballads*, Boston, 1892–8.

Chronicles of Croyland, ed. Henry Riley, London, 1893.

Christ Church Letters, ed. J.B. Sheppard, Camden Society, 1877.

Davies, Robert, *Extracts from the Municipal Records of the City of York*, London, 1843.

Excerpta Historica, ed. S. Bentley, London, 1831.

Halliwell, J.O., *Letters of the Kings of England*, London, 1846.

Historie of the Arrivall of Edward IV in England, ed. John Bruce, Camden Society, 1838.

Leland, John, *Collectanea*, 6 vols, ed. Thomas Hearne, London, 1774.

Letters and Papers Illustrative of the Reigns of Richard III and Henry VII, ed. James Gairdner, 2 vols, Rolls Series, London, 1861–3.

Mancini, Dominic, *The Usurpation of Richard III*, ed. C.A.J. Armstrong, Oxford, 1936.

Monstrelet, E. de, *Chroniques*, 15 vols, ed. Jean Buchon, Paris, 1826–7.

Paston Letters, ed. James Gairdner, 6 vols, London, 1910.

Percy, Thomas, *Bishop Percy's Folio Manuscript*, ed. J.W. Hales and E.J. Furnivall, 3 vols, London, 1867–8.

Political Poems and Songs relating to English History, vol. 2, ed. Thomas Wright, Rolls Series, London, 1861.

Rolls of Parliament, vol. 6, Edward IV–Henry VII, London, 1783.

Rous, John, *The Rous Roll*, ed. William Courthope, London, 1859.

Rymer, Thomas, *Foedera*, vols 11 and 12, London, 1727.

Stonor Letters and Papers, 1290–1483, ed. C.L. Kingsford, 2 vols, Camden Society, 1919.

Warkworth, John, *A Chronicle of the First Thirteen Years of the Reign of King Edward IV*, ed. J.O. Halliwell, Camden Society, 1839.

Whethamstede, John, *Register*, ed. Henry Riley, Rolls Series, London, 1872.

Worcester, William of, *Annals*, Rolls Series, London, 1864.

TUDOR SOURCES

Fabyan, Robert, *The New Chronicles of England and France*, ed. Henry Ellis, London, 1811.

Grafton, Richard, *Chronicle*, ed. Henry Ellis, 2 vols, 1809.

Great Chronicle of London, ed. A.H. Thomas and I.D. Thornley, London, 1938.

Hardyng, John, *Chronicles*, ed. Henry Ellis, London, 1812.

Holinshed, Raphael, *Chronicles*, ed. Henry Ellis, 6 vols, London, 1807–8.

More, Sir Thomas, *The History of King Richard III*, ed. J.R. Lumby, Cambridge, 1883.

Rastell, John, *Pastyme of Peoples*, ed. James Dibdin, London, 1811.

Rous, John, *Historia Regum Angliae*, ed. Thomas Hearne, Oxford, 1716.

Stowe, John, *Annales of England*, London, 1615.

Vergil, Polydore, *English History*, ed. Henry Ellis, Camden Society, 1844.

LATER WRITERS

Bacon, Francis, *History of the Reign of Henry VII*, ed. J.R. Lumby, London, 1885.

Baker, Richard, *Chronicle of the Kings of England*, London, 1643.

Buck, George, *History of the Life and Reigne of Richard III*, London, 1647.

Campbell, William, *Materials for a History of the Reign of Henry VII*, 2 vols, Rolls Series, London, 1873, 1877.

Carte, Thomas, *General History of England*, vol. 2, London, 1750.

Cokayne, G.E., *The Complete Peerage*, 14 vols, London, 1910–59.

Cornwallis, Sir William, 'The Praise of Richard III', *Somers Tracts*, ed. Walter Scott, vol. 3, 1810, pp. 316–28.

Courtenay, T.P., *Commentaries on the Historical Plays of Shakespeare*, 2 vols, London, 1840.

Drake, Francis, *Eboracum: History and Antiquities of the City of York*, London, 1736.

Gairdner, James, *History of the Life and Reign of Richard III*, London, 1898.

—— *Henry VII*, London, 1889.

—— *The Houses of Lancaster and York*, London, 1875.

Habington, William, *The Historie of Edward the Fourth*, London, 1640.

Halsted, Caroline, *Richard III as Duke of Gloucester and King of England*, 2 vols, London, 1844.

Henry, Robert, *The History of Great Britain* (with Laing's appendix), vols 7–12, London, 1823.

Hume, David, *History of England to 1688*, 8 vols, London, 1789.

Jesse, J.H., *Memoirs of Richard III*, London, 1862.

Kendall, P.M., *Richard the Third*, London, 1955.

Kingsford, C.L., *English Historical Literature in the Fifteenth Century*, Oxford, 1913.

Legge, A.O., *The Unpopular King: the Life and Times of Richard III*, 2 vols, London, 1885.

Lindsay, Philip, *On Some Bones in Westminster Abbey*, London, 1934.

Lingard, John, *History of England*, 6th ed. 10 vols, London, 1854–5.

Markham, Clements R., *Richard III: his Life and Character*, London, 1906.

Oman, Charles, *History of England, 1377–1485*, London, 1906.

Ramsay, James, *Lancaster and York*, 2 vols, Oxford, 1892.

Rapin-Thoyras, Paul de, *History of England*, 13 vols, translated by N. Tindal, London, 1757–60.

Sandford, Francis, *Genealogical History of the Kings of England*, London, 1707.

Scofield, Cora, *The Life and Reign of Edward the Fourth*, 2 vols, London, 1923.

Stubbs, William, *Constitutional History of England*, 3 vols, Oxford, 1873.

Tanner, Lawrence, and Wright, William, 'Recent Investigations regarding the Fate of the Princes in the Tower', *Archaeologia*, vol. 84, 1935, pp. 1–26.

Turner, Sharon, *The History of England during the Middle Ages*, vols 3–4, London, 1830.

Walpole, Horace, *Historic Doubts on the Life and Reign of King Richard III*, London, 1767.

PART TWO: RECENT BOOKS AND NEW EDITIONS

British Library Harleian Manuscript 433, ed. Rosemary Horrox and P.W. Hammond, 4 vols, Upminster and London, 1979–83.

Buck, George, *The History of King Richard the Third*, ed. A.N. Kincaid, Gloucester, 1979.

Chrimes, S.B., *Henry VII*, London, 1972.

Commynes, Philippe de, *Memoirs: the Reign of Louis XI, 1461–1483*, ed. Michael Jones, London, 1972.

Crowland Chronicle Continuations 1459–1486, ed. Nicholas Pronay and John Cox, London, 1986.

Encomium of Richard III by Sir William Cornwallis the Younger, ed. A.N. Kincaid, London, 1977.

Gransden, Antonia, *Historical Writing in England, Volume 2: c. 1307 to Early Sixteenth Century*, London, 1982.

Griffiths, R.A., *The Reign of King Henry VI*, London, 1981.

Hammond, P.W., and Sutton, Anne F., *Richard III: the Road to Bosworth Field*, London, 1985.

Hanham, Alison, *Richard III and his early historians, 1483–1535*, Oxford, 1975.

Horrox, Rosemary, *Richard III: a Study of Service*, Cambridge, 1989.

Mancini, Dominic, *The Usurpation of Richard III*, ed. C.A.J. Armstrong, 2nd ed., Oxford, 1969.

More, Thomas, *The History of King Richard III*, ed. R.S. Sylvester, Yale, 1967.

Potter, Jeremy, *Good King Richard?*, London, 1983.

Raine, Angelo, *York Civic Records*, vol. 1, Yorkshire Archaeological Society Record Series, 1939.

Ross, Charles, *Edward IV*, London, 1974.

Ross, Charles, *Richard III*, London, 1981.
—— *Wars of the Roses*, London, 1976.
Walpole, Horace, *Historic Doubts on the Life and Reign of King Richard the Third* (with introduction and notes by P.W. Hammond), Gloucester, 1987.

INDEX

All personal names are indexed, with kings and queens, princes and sovereign dukes under first name and peers and bishops under title, with a cross reference from the family name.